May all your Christmases
be joyful!

Kathryn Holley Seibel

THE JOYFUL CHRISTMAS

CRAFT BOOK

THE JOYFUL CHRISTMAS CRAFT BOOK

KATHRYN HOLLEY SEIBEL

Photographs by
WILLIAM E. SEIBEL

D. VAN NOSTRAND COMPANY, INC.

PRINCETON, NEW JERSEY
TORONTO
NEW YORK
LONDON

D. VAN NOSTRAND COMPANY, INC.
120 Alexander St., Princeton, New Jersey (*Principal office*)
24 West 40 Street, New York 18, New York

D. VAN NOSTRAND COMPANY, LTD.
358, Kensington High Street, London, W.14, England

D. VAN NOSTRAND COMPANY (Canada), LTD.
25 Hollinger Road, Toronto 16, Canada

Published simultaneously in Canada by
D. VAN NOSTRAND COMPANY (Canada), LTD.

PRINTED IN THE UNITED STATES OF AMERICA

Preface

To Know The Joy of Christmas

THE CHRISTMAS CELEBRATION, unique in the history of the world, touches everyone, Christian and non-Christian, in a personal, often poignant, way. It commemorates the birth of the Christ Child some two thousand years ago in the lowly stable in Bethlehem where Mary and Joseph took refuge when there was no room at the inn. The brightest star this world has ever seen shone upon the stable. Inside, on a bed of straw, lay the newborn King. The gentle lowing of the cattle was His cradle song. The cattle and all things inside the shed reflected His great golden glory. The events of that holy night have so impressed the world that each common element in the stable has become a symbol of Christmas—the ox and ass, the doves, the manger, the straw, and the shed itself.

Add to these, the angels and celestial voices singing, the wise men, the shepherds and the sheep, the star, the radiance; the three figures of The Babe, Mary, and Joseph; the secular aspects associated with home—Santa Claus, gifts, mistletoe, poinsettias, greeting cards, feasting, log fires, hot punch, popcorn, fruit, and nuts; the family together; a sense of personal peace and joy beyond description.

The celebration of Christmas is a tradition without geographical boundaries. The telling and retelling of the story in many languages, in many countries, cities, villages, and hamlets, in mansion and cottage, has dignified it as the greatest story ever told. One of the awesome aspects of this age-old tradition is that the simple facts of Christ's birth, told and retold in diverse languages and in millions of versions for nearly two thousand years, have never lost their impact. Each year the account is fresh and powerful. Each year we feel its tug at our heartstrings.

There are as many ways of telling the story as there are people to tell it. In some homes it is the mother who gathers the children about her at bedtime to read or narrate the story, illustrating it with the children's own toys, or with nativity figures cherished from year to year, perhaps made by the parents themselves. These have the deepest meaning. No matter how crudely they are fashioned, they are tangible proof of the parents' love. Later in life, it may be the memory of these simple things that draws a man or woman home for Christmas, no matter how many hundreds of miles must be traveled.

Christmas means something wonderfully different to each of us. In the United States, the diversity of our ancestry is at once the cause and the delight of our own particular celebration. The proximity of immigrants from many countries and the exchange of customs have enriched the texture and colored the fabric of our American Christmas to make it unique. There is no "proper" pattern of celebration here, as there is in England. Here we blend the English traditions with German, Italian, Polish, Bohemian, Greek, French, Scandinavian, and all the rest.

Some years ago in our Ohio town, which is near the steel mills of Cleveland, there was a very small and rather solemn boy with great black eyes and a voice as big as a man's. His mother was Welsh; his father Polish. When we asked him an oft-repeated question, "Andy, what are you?" he would throw back his shoulders and bellow in his deep voice, "I'm a Welsh Polack."

And what are we all? French-Norwegian, English-Greek, Swedish-Bohemian, Spanish-Italian? Or have we so many ancestral strains that we are simply United States American?

And what constitutes a truly American Christmas? In many cities, first- and second-generation nationality groups gather to celebrate Christmas as they did in the "old country." But gradually these customs are changed as nationalities intermarry and the children at school are exposed to different traditions. They want to say their *Merry Christmas* the American way.

Depending on locality, this desire is expressed in various ways. In Cleveland there is the influence of the outdoor lighting displays of the General Electric Company's Nela Park. For several decades this has attracted hundreds of thousands of people through the Christmas season. Those who like such a display now decorate their homes with similar and often extravagant lighting. Ranch-type homes with wide roof lines blaze with garlands of lights that outline eves, windows, doors, and set pieces on lawn and roof—Santas climbing into chimneys, sleighs and reindeer, greetings spelled out by electricity. On many lawns, there is a lighted crèche, and passersby sometimes are startled to see live animals feeding on hay. Prizes are awarded in suburbs for the most artistic displays, and these awards usually go to those exhibits that have good design, and but one or two colors effectively used.

Over-generosity is an American characteristic—and a great pitfall. "If a little is good, more is better!" But many appreciate the value of restraint and find that though extremes may get the most public attention, the appeal is apt to be short-lived. Extravagance burns itself out. Thus, our best American traditions evolve.

Each Christmas many of us search diligently for the unique in decorations, gifts, and greeting cards. We make mental notes for next Christmas, and then are seldom satisfied with the decorations we pull out of storeroom or attic; we add to and subtract from these each year. We discard the fad and keep the precious. The things we consider good are thus preserved and become traditional and some day may find their way to museums.

The wonderful thing about the Christmas celebration here is that it is ever growing and evolving. Individually and industrially, it is newly created each year; yet essentially it remains Christmas. And it is inconceivable that our traditions should ever become set. If they did, it would mean the end of our creativity, and the decline of our industrial well-being.

In this twentieth century when machine mass production is the order of the day, we are apt to deny ourselves the joy and privilege of expressing ourselves in handmade decorations, gifts, and greeting cards. We may want to but feel uncertain. Lacking ideas or know-how, we falter. What a pity! For this twentieth century is also producing marvelous materials for our use—attractive papers, foils, wood veneers, thin metals, plastics, glass bottles, woven and printed fabrics. Even the supermarkets offer countless foodstuffs for us to use in decorative ways. Cars and airplanes bring us curious natural products from distant lands, fascinating seed pods, shells, and plants, as well as woodwork from Germany, paper products from Poland and Japan, strawcraft from Sweden, and basketry from Hong Kong.

This book is therefore dedicated to all of you who want to experience the great joy of using these rich opportunities to make your own Christmas decorations, gifts, and greeting cards. Through the use of your individual talents, each of you may measure out your own portion of Christmas happiness. May you all know this true joy of making and giving, and each year create your own personal and glorious Merry Christmas.

KATHRYN HOLLEY SEIBEL

Brecksville, Ohio
August 1963

In Appreciation

It is with a grateful heart that I express my thanks to friends and relatives who so generously gave their help and moral support while this book was being prepared.

I am especially indebted to the Cleveland Museum of Art and to the Cleveland Institute of Art for their educational courses and exhibits.

Contents

List of Illustrations

IN COLOR

IN BLACK AND WHITE

ILLUSTRATIONS

xvi

1

Paper for
Christmas Decorations

Paper is an excellent and inexpensive material for Christmas decorations, and you may have enough right in the house to do a most imaginative job. A wallpaper sample book in your attic (or from a local decorator) alone can do it, or newspapers and wrapping paper can be covered with casein wall paint and used in many ways. Colored pages from magazines are a help. Paper cups of various shapes, paper towels, facial tissues, waxed paper, and corrugated paper boxes can all be put to use. The purchase of a little art paper will go far toward really splendid decorations and be fine for your Christmas cards, too.

FOR STORM DOOR OR WINDOW

STAINED-GLASS WITH WAXED PAPER

A roll of waxed paper, some stubs of wax crayons, and a warm iron can convert your glass storm sash into a "stained-glass" window, pleasant with daylight sifting through, lovely at night when the house lights shine behind it to greet the passerby with a Christmas message in warm, bright colors (Color Plate II). The children can help with this project. If there are small panes in your storm door, measure them carefully and let the children cut two sheets of waxed paper slightly larger than each pane. If your door has two large panes, use narrow black masking tape to divide them into small sections or into irregular spaces like those in a church window.

While you are working on this project, protect the table with newspapers. Experiment with some small pieces of waxed paper to test the heat of the iron and its effect on the crayon. Shave wax crayons with a paring knife onto separate pieces of paper, keeping the colors well separated. Choose just two colors to start with, and use more of one than the other. Cover a small piece of paper with the shaved crayons, place a second piece over the shavings, hold a warm iron on the paper *for a few seconds only,* then gently lift the iron. To prevent a total blending of color, do not slide the iron. Your own selection of colors and your technique of lifting the iron will produce a design.

Some design control is possible, as experimenting will show. Try using several shades of green crayon, and with a knife blade maneuver the shavings into the form of a tree, bird, or star. A few yellow or orange crayon chips will brighten a green tree. Pale blue flecked with white will look like sky.

When trying to control a design, be sure the iron is at its lowest point of heat, and let it remain only a second or two on the paper. For fine points in a design, use only the tip of the iron. Another control method is to lay a glued thread around the outline of a design to keep the crayon colors separated.

When you combine stars, angels, birds, and other Christmas motifs for your Christmas door, use some of the same colors in each section, though in different amounts, to unify the composition.

STAINED-GLASS EFFECTS WITH OILED PAPER

In contrast to the waxed-paper technique, very clean-cut black-edged designs are possible with oiled paper. A pad of white art paper is recommended; however, any

3

1. STORM-DOOR DECORATION. A stained-glass effect is achieved with wax crayons and a black Magic Marker on oiled paper.

kind of heavy unmarked paper, such as shelf or wrapping paper, may be used. A teaspoonful of linseed, salad, or baby oil may be enough for each sheet. With your finger-tips, rub it into the paper thoroughly and evenly until all the opaque white disappears and the paper becomes translucent. With cloth or paper towel, polish the paper until all excess oil is removed. Then place on newspapers overnight to dry.

Simple designs are best. On white paper, draw a thumbnail plan of the door or window you wish to decorate. Consider whether the space is large or small, and plan your design to suit it. As a suggestion, place identical triangles on each space or circles of varying size, or overlap diamond shapes.

Unlike waxed paper, oiled paper will take a pencil mark. When you have planned your design, draw or trace it onto the oiled paper with pencil. Then go over the pencil lines with a marking pen (Magic Marker or Sanford's Marker) to produce uniform, thick, black lines like those in a leaded window. This kind of marking is quickly and easily done.

When the leaded marking is finished, plan a color scheme to resemble a stained glass window. Rub 1-inch pieces of wax crayon horizontally over the oiled paper, blending two or three colors onto the same area. Some

5

areas might be left without color. Then the effect will be dainty when the drawing is held up to the light. To increase intensity of hue, rub both sides of the paper with the same color.

Rubber cement is the best adhesive to hold waxed or oiled papers to glass.

COLORED OILED PAPER

Construction paper in bright colors is available at art-supply stores and may be oiled as explained above. It is excellent to convert windows into translucent stained glass. No crayoning is necessary. Simply plan a design on a sheet of wrapping paper the size of the window. Work from a well-designed Christmas card, if you wish, enlarging to fit the window. When your color plan is finished, trace and cut the pieces. Use a black Magic Marker to edge each piece, then attach to the window with rubber cement and you will have a very striking effect.

PAPER-TOWEL ART FOR MANTELS AND WALLS

The household paper towel may be used as art paper for children's projects or for your own decorating schemes. It often substitutes in art classes for expensive

6

papers. Advantage is taken of its capacity to absorb water. Imaginative youngsters sponge or brush water colors onto paper towels to produce color fantasies of fairy-tale quality.

For these effects, the paper towel may be premoistened so that the applied colors run helter-skelter. Controlled effects can be produced on dry towels. A dry sponge or brush lightly touching dry paper with color will bring out the texture of the towel, and many effects are possible.

For Christmas, let the children decorate the family or recreation room with illustrations of favorite Christmas stories on paper towels. Lines may be drawn with crayon, chalk, or ink, but the coloring should be sponged or brushed on. A child could make an experimental sample sheet to see how many different effects are possible, then plan a series of pictures using them. A long scroll like a Japanese scroll can be made of a yard of paper towels, untorn, and hung with a small dowel tacked top and bottom.

Because paper towels are soft and opaque, they are fine for snowflake cutouts, to decorate a mantel. Study your mantel and plan your effects accordingly. Large and small snowflakes might be used, or all of one size could be placed in a tilelike border on the face of the mantel. If the space above is of dark wood or colored paint or

7

paper, opaque white snowflakes will stand out nicely. If the wall is white, a backing of geometric cut-outs of colored construction paper behind the snowflakes will produce a striking effect.

How to Cut a Snowflake

Snowflakes are always six-pointed designs. Measure and cut the largest square possible from a paper towel and discard the excess. Fold the square in half, then measure and mark the exact center of the fold. Next, fold into diagonal thirds, radiating from the marked central point (as you might fold a pocket handkerchief). Crease carefully so as not to stretch the paper. Start cutting the design at the tip of the fold, removing a small section. Cut the next piece from the opposite side. Each cut-out piece will be somewhat larger than the last. No pattern is followed exactly, as no two snow crystals are ever the same. Each paper snowflake is a surprise to the freehand artist with a sharp scissors.

Snowflake Enlarged

A very large snowflake can be made by enlarging a small design and drawing a section of it onto heavy construction paper, white or colored. Cut with a large scissors. An exciting abstraction results (Fig. 2). Use rubber cement as adhesive.

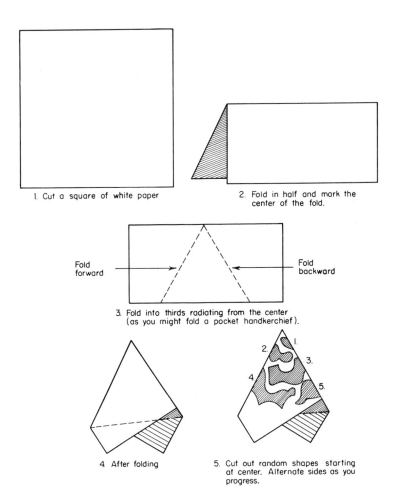

1. Cut a square of white paper

2. Fold in half and mark the center of the fold.

Fold forward → ← Fold backward

3. Fold into thirds radiating from the center (as you might fold a pocket handkerchief).

4. After folding

5. Cut out random shapes starting at center. Alternate sides as you progress.

Note: Circles of paper may also be folded and cut in this way.

DIRECTIONS FOR CUTTING A PAPER SNOWFLAKE

9

2. PAPER TOWELS AND CONSTRUCTION PAPER FOR A MODERN DESIGN. Paper-towel snowflakes give a tilelike effect to the face of this mantel with an enlarged snowflake, cut and reassembled, to make an abstract design on the wall above. Two clay winter birds complete the composition. This plan could be carried out in bright colors.

CORRUGATED BOXBOARD FOR A STABLE

A stable can be easily constructed with two pieces of corrugated boxboard. One strip, 2½ inches wide by 17 inches long, is scored and bent 6¾ inches from one end to make the off-center peak of the roof. This allows the base to spread to about 14 inches. To make the back, place this angled section on its side on another piece of corrugated board and trace the triangle with a pencil; then cut it out. Secure the triangle for the back wall to the roof with glued brown-paper strips, folded lengthwise in half, and attached inside (Fig. 3).

Make roof shingles from pine-cone scales. Start at the base and glue them on, row after row, allowing the glue

3. Corrugated Paper Construction for a Stable. Design by William E. Seibel.

to dry a few minutes after each row. Quick-drying Elmer's Glue-All is better than mucilage for this purpose. If you wish, mount the stable on a base of corrugated board cut to fit your mantel and cover the base with burlap. Paste a piece of the same burlap inside the stable. To hide the corrugations at the roof edge, glue a piece of small dowel or straw to the edge. Use one straw to support the gold star at the back of the stable.

Creche Figures

Imported, well-designed figures depicting the Nativity can now be purchased in many shops for about a dollar a set. Those in Fig. 4 were made in Italy and stand about 3 inches high; all are contained in a package about the size of a box of animal crackers. Though small, when these are set up, the composition is effective enough for a Christmas mantelpiece.

PAPER-CUP CREATIONS FOR CHILDREN

Today's craftsman takes advantage of ready-made precision-cut shapes to produce clean-cut results with the least effort. Paper cups are well constructed and inexpensive. Many kinds are available at soda fountains and supermarkets, and in some homes there are paper-cup dispensers in kitchen or bathroom.

4. STABLE WITH PINE-CONE SHINGLES. Small wood figures from Italy complete this scene with a crèche for a Christmas mantel.

Tall and short figures for Christmas decorating can be made from cone-shaped paper cups. With these, Nativity figures are easily fashioned. For the heads, attach papier-mâché, Styrofoam, or wooden balls to pipe cleaners, and insert them through a tiny hole at the point of the cup. Cover the cups with colored construction paper,

13

suede paper, felt, velvet, or cloth. Make arms with pipe cleaners. No sewing is necessary; Elmer's Glue-All is a good adhesive (Fig. 5). Trim with gold braid, velvet ribbon, Lacelon, or sequins.

For a children's party, make a table-sized tree of paper cups with flat bases. Cover with white construction paper and decorate with Christmas card cut-outs. As you search through old Christmas cards, sort out figures that will suit the space on the cup without crowding. A flying angel, for instance, should have plenty of space to fly in.

Ten cups will make a pyramid tree. Each may be decorated with gold-paper strips at top and bottom, and the top cup can support a star. The reverse side of each cup may also be decorated with shapes cut from Christmas cards. If the same shape (a tree or star) is used, make each one of a different paper for variety (Fig. 6, Color Plate IV). When the children have finished refreshments, give each child a cup with a surprise gift wrapped and hidden inside it.

ORNAMENTS FOR TREES AND MOBILES

Mobiles and trees may be decorated completely with homemade paper ornaments. Wallpaper sample books are an excellent source of printed designs that can be

5. PAPER CUPS FOR NATIVITY FIGURES. Paper cups are covered with blue, white, and brown paper and trimmed with Lacelon and gold braid. Heads are made of wooden beads; hands and manger of popsickle sticks and a pint berry box.

15

6. PYRAMID TREE OF PAPER CUPS. Flat-bottomed paper cups are decorated with Christmas card cut-outs. Backs are also decorated, and each cup holds a hidden gift.

converted into three-dimensional ornaments. Most wall-paper manufacturers or dealers are glad to have their out-dated sample books used by customers. Many of these books are printed in tan, brown, gold, pink, blue and white with extra pages of plain matching colors. These may be used for your own three-dimensional stars, snow-flakes, angels, and abstract shapes.

Cut out three similar printed shapes but in different colors to make a three-dimensional design. Crease the center line of each one. For a hanger, glue both ends of a loop of thread to the center of one of the shapes and allow to dry. Cover one half of the first shape with white glue or paste, and place half of the second one on the pasted part. Next, paste the third shape entirely to the remaining parts of the first and second. Decorate edges with glitter or sequins. If the ornament is large, sequins may be glued here and there to the design to make it sparkle as it moves. You could base the color scheme for your Christmas decorating on the wallpaper colors you choose for your tree.

Similar four-sided ornaments can be made with two double-faced cut-outs. Slit each ornament halfway down to the center; then slide the ornaments together at right angles.

Cone-shaped paper cups may also be used for three-dimensional ornaments. First, pierce the tip end of one of the cups and insert a knotted thread for a hanger. Glue the edge of an identical cup to the first cup, holding them together with spring-type clothes pins or hair clips until the glue dries. Then paint or cover with gay wrapping paper, foil, sequins, and glitter.

CHRISTMAS CARDS

WITH STENCILS

Each Christmas new ideas and new tricks prove the versatility and timeless virtues of stenciling. This will never be old-fashioned so long as imagination is at work. The old method produced a spotty effect that we recognized at once as stenciling. Now with a better understanding of design, we find we can produce good two- and three-color work that looks like expensive printing. Even one-color stencils are attractive when modern simplified designs are followed (Color Plate I).

Use EZCut transparent stencil paper made by the American Crayon Company for quick and easy cutting. Or make your own stencil paper by shredding paraffin over heavy art or wrapping paper and pressing with a warm iron. The paper will absorb the paraffin. Freezer paper also makes a fairly good stencil. A sharp stencil knife gives best results.

7. DUTCH CHRISTMAS CARDS. Designed and printed on cloth by Corry Erkens of Utrecht, these are good examples of appropriate stencils.

Inexpensive art or construction paper is the best to buy for Christmas cards to be stenciled. It is easily folded and takes paint or mimeograph ink very well.

Tree designs are excellent and stylized forms easy to do. Sketch a tree with pencil on ordinary paper or cut it out with scissors, whichever is easier. Make the outer line or silhouette simple and straight; inner branches can be patterned. Trace and cut your design from stencil paper. A pointed razor-blade knife from an art store is the best tool.

Water or tempera colors may be used for the stenciling. If your cards are of colored paper, try white tempera paint for the stenciling. Use the dry-brush technique—a stiff bristle brush is immersed in paint and then squeezed dry. It will retain most of the pigment and, brushed onto paper, produce a rough, dry texture instead of the more familiar smooth, painted finish. This way the paint never runs under the stencil and dries almost immediately. To produce a halo, brush outward at right angles over the edges of a shape. The effect will be that of light shining behind a silhouette.

If you prefer the stencil knife to paint, simply cut and paste designs directly onto the folded cards. Use both inner and outer cut-outs for interesting effects.

WITH MAGAZINE CUT-OUTS

A sharp scissors, a little imagination, and bright colored ads from current magazines are all you need for a new kind of greeting card, which is really note paper. Gifts made this way are bound to amuse your friends (Color Plate III).

Gift note paper may be purchased with envelopes at little cost. When decorated, it will have a personal quality long remembered. Cut any shapes you wish—chickens, geese, birds, fish, or abstracts—from white paper. Freely cut out designs with scissors until the forms please you. When you have cut several that compose well on the size note paper you have chosen, you are ready to go into production. With a paper clip, clamp the white pattern onto three or four thicknesses of cut-up colored ads, and repeat until you have at least a dozen of each shape. This will give you many colors to choose from when you compose the separate sheets. Be sure edges are cut smooth and true. A sharp-pointed embroidery scissors is best for this purpose.

White notepaper is recommended. A dozen sheets may be composed at the same time by laying them out on a table. Each will be different in color and design or both. Choose from your cut-outs colors that go well together.

You may wish to combine warm hues—yellow, orange, red—on one sheet, and cool hues—blue, green, purple— on another; or, you may prefer contrasting colors. When all the sheets are composed, fasten the pieces neatly in place with Elmer's Glue-All spread on with a toothpick. Eyes, legs, feet, and tail feathers may be drawn on with black ink.

Christmas cards with abstractions or realistic cut-outs are made the same way, a dozen at a time. The important point is to cut a design from white paper first. Look through last year's Christmas cards for easy-to-cut silhouettes of wise men, trees, and so on.

WITH OLD STAMPS

If you are a saver of stamps that come in the daily mail, you will have plenty to use for original Christmas cards. Buy construction paper and ready-made envelopes at a stationery store, and plan a Christmas-tree card of cut-up postage stamps or Christmas seals. Paste odd stamps or pieces of stamps inside the outline of your design. The variety of color will make each card interesting.

8. A SANTA CLAUS MONTAGE. Cut-outs from greeting cards dated 1950 to 1960 are mounted on pasteboard and framed in wood.

WAX-EMBOSSING FOR CHRISTMAS CARDS

A delightful surprise is in store for you if you make your own distinctive Christmas papers for cards or wrapping with a wax-embossing technique. It produces a soft, pliable paper that is most attractive. The slightly raised texture invites the touch. Held to the light, it is translucent. Held over white paper, it seems to glow.

To experiment, tear off a 6-inch piece of freezer paper and cut it into squares. Cover each square, wax side up, with shaved crayons: (1) red and gold, (2) green and gold, (3) red and green, as you wish. Hold a slightly warm iron over the first square *directly on the shavings* for just a few seconds. The wax will melt and cover the paper. Quickly lift off the iron, allowing most of the wax to remain. This will create a raised pattern of two colors slightly blended. When the paper cools, the wax will be hard and the paper ready for use. The resulting paper is soft and workable, beautiful on both sides.

While the iron is still warm, clean it with a soft cloth before working with a second group of colors. Don't worry about your iron. The wax improves the ironing surface. But *do* clean it thoroughly while it is still warm to remove all traces of color and wax.

24

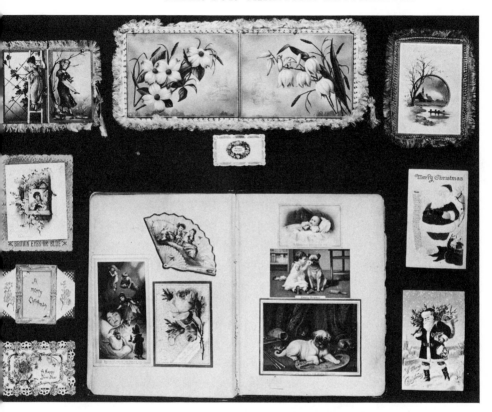

9. ANTIQUE CHRISTMAS CARDS. The names of Prang, Tuck, and Kate Greenaway marked the Christmas cards of 1850 to 1890. Note the sentiment, the predominance of floral motifs, lace, and fringe, but Santa is still Santa. From the collection of Mrs. Irene Strong, Marshall, Michigan.

This paper can be used for stained-glass effects on Christmas cards. Cut the face of a folded card with a stencil knife to make a frame; then attach the embossed paper underneath the frame. Or, cut the paper into tree, star, or abstract shapes and attach to white or colored construction paper folded to make a greeting card. The addition of hand-cut gold paper stars of your own original design will give these cards distinction.

Workshop Fun With Paper

1. If you are a collector of theatre ticket stubs, liquor labels, match cases, motel soap wrappers, or maps, here is a use for them. Round up all your old metal or cardboard waste baskets and spray them with gold paint. Then decorate the outside with designs made of one collection or another. Use quick-drying glue, dry, and spray with clear lacquer.
2. *Gift Idea*: Decorate new wastebaskets with unusual, imaginative paper cut-outs or maps. Lacquer to preserve.
3. Decorate new wastebaskets with 1/4-inch cross sections of paper tubes. Use them as daisy centers with cardboard petals glued into designs, or use them to make abstract designs. Best designs have a variety of sizes, with the largest in a prominent place. Spray all over with gold.

4. *Gift for a Child*: Decorate round, pint ice-cream cartons, washed and carefully dried, with magazine cut-outs and unmatched letters spelling the child's name. Fill with new crayons.

5. *Gift for Mother*: Using the same kind of cartons, decorate with magazine cut-outs of scissors, spools of thread, needles, and so on; fill the box with new spools of thread, thimble, package of needles, and embroidery scissors. Lacquer the outside of the box.

6. *Gift for Father*: Cover match cases or tiny match boxes neatly with gold-foil paper, then cut out unmatched letters from a colored magazine ad to form his name. (Or make personalized place cards for a party the same way.)

7. Make large Christmas ornaments of laundry-box cardboard cut into 12-inch circles, triangles, ovals, and diamonds. Cut two for each ornament. Trace a stencil design on each one, allowing for $\frac{1}{2}$-inch band between the cut-out pieces. Cut identical stencils on matching shapes. Spray with gold. Use crayoned oiled, waxed, or embossed waxed paper, described previously, to sandwich between the two layers of cut-out cardboard. Glue together, using spring clothespins to hold until dry. Attach gold or red cord for hanging each ornament.

8. Look around the house for cardboard tubes of different sizes from bathroom tissue, paper-towel rolls, crochet-cotton spools. Cut into ½-inch sections. Paint with gold. Cut ½-inch by 10-inch strips of red or turquoise construction paper, and curl the paper at each end over a piece of dowel. Insert the curls into each tube. Try one, two, and three curls in large tubes to make designs. Using different length strips, make designs inside and outside the tubes, gluing or stapling the ends. Hang as tree ornaments or make a mobile of them.

9. *For the Children*: Make a Mexican piñata—or gift-filled balloon—with a large round balloon. Inflate and cover it completely with ½-inch strips of newspaper dipped in liquid laundry starch. Allow to dry for a day or two. In one end, cut a hole about the size of your fist, and make a hanger of strong cord with ends knotted inside the ball. Cover the ball with rosettes of colored facial tissue, tied with heavy thread and glued to the surface. If two colors are used, make a spiral or circular design of them. The ball may be made into a bird or chicken by adding a head and tail of construction paper. Fill the ball with small gifts, and hang up in the center of a room.

10. For easy-to-make Christmas cards, cut several sheets of various colored facial tissue into tree-shaped triangles of three sizes. Apply a thin coat of starch or glue to each triangle and arrange in a design on folded Chistmas card paper. The charm of this will be the embossed effect of the crinkled tissue as it dries on the card. Add bits of glitter if you wish.

2

Decorating with Foodstuffs

Christmas plans often start in the kitchen. Here all manner of spices and herbs, figs, dates and nuts, raisins and currants, and bottles of flavoring fill the cupboard shelves in anticipation of the first day of Christmas baking.

Years ago in my English mother's kitchen, the big preparations began in October when the Baldwin apples were ripe, and sisters and aunts got together to make the mincemeat. They pared apples, bushels of them, for hours, and then mixed the spices, raisins and currants with the chopped fruit, ground beef suet off the kidney, and plenty of brown sugar. Mixing was done with hands and arms up to the elbow and in the largest crocks available. There was no recipe, just a handful of this and of that with much critical sampling, until all agreed the flavor was just right. Last came the brandy, for taste and preservation—a cupful over the top of each family's level crockful. The mincemeat took weeks to season in the coldest part of the cellar, the crocks tightly covered with plates weighted with heavy stones. By Christmas, it was at its peak. The plum puddings and fruit cakes were made next. Everyone knew that they too were best after a couple of months of aging.

Quantity was important, for there were others to consider beside the family, like our Czechoslovakian neighbor who always stopped by with a gift of kolachy, cookies filled with prunes, cheese, poppy seeds, or ground nuts. A mince pie made a nice exchange. Neighbors with German or Polish specialties came too, each proud of an old-country recipe. Each went home smiling with a fruit cake or a pudding. It all took planning.

Today we store our Christmas cookies, pies, and holiday breads and desserts in a freezer, and our recipes are often of international origin. Artistic talent will be apparent in many of these creations—pies decorated with pastry designs and edgings cut, fluted, or braided to suit. A Christmas stollen, two feet long, may be braided and trimmed with candied cherries and fruits and icing to make a centerpiece for the Christmas Eve table. Cookies may be miniature jewels or larger storybook figures painted with colored icing in fine detail, right down to the eyelashes.

Eighteenth-Century Christmas

In Virginia at Colonial Williamsburg, visitors at Christmas time enjoy authentic eighteenth-century customs, foods, and decorations. Festivities begin a week beforehand and continue until New Year's Day. At dusk each evening, a white candle is lighted in every window in the village, making a beautiful Christmas picture. The stranger feels a warm glow of welcome and enjoys a sense of peace and comfort. Doorways are decked with wreaths of greens and fresh fruits. Apples, lemons, limes, grapes, pears, pineapples, and pomegranates are arranged in designs to suit each one.

Visitors can step back two centuries to feast sumptuously at Christiana Campbell's Tavern, where the Christmas party lasts three hours. It is properly called *The Groaning Board.* Hostesses in eighteenth-century costume greet them at the door and they might almost expect to see Christiana Campbell herself, "a little old woman about four feet high and equally thick, with a little turn-up pug nose." As the yard-square napkins are tied about their necks, the twentieth-century disappears.

A huge mug of ale is served each guest, and kept filled throughout the party. A cup of hot mulled cider arrives simultaneously with the ballad singers, and guitars and violins strike up merry Christmas tunes. The fried trout and piping hot spoon bread are almost overlooked as guests join in the carols. With joy and gusto, everyone sings in full voice, "Deck the Halls," "Joy to the World," "God Rest Ye Merry, Gentlemen."

When the music stops for a moment, food is served— roast beef that melts on the tongue, potato balls, creamed onions with chopped peanuts, green beans, hot biscuits, luscious corn bread with butter. After each course, another round of singing. Salad is served with spicy sweet potato pancakes and game pie. Coffee. Mince pie with cheese. Flaming plum pudding with brandied sauce. Every mouthful the more delicious and flavored with spirited music as strangers join together in joyous songfest and feast, all happily proclaiming the birthday of the Lord.

DECORATING WITH FRUIT

The wreaths, swags, and table pieces made with fresh fruits that decorated colonial homes look well in homes today. Simple in design and bold in form, they are in keeping with contemporary decoration. Certainly the wonderful fragrance of fresh fruit cannot be duplicated. Fresh fruit is attractive to all, to the small child, to the grandfather, who might not notice a decoration of artificial fruit. And visitors will exclaim, "It smells so good in this house . . . it must be the fruit."

TECHNIQUES WITH FRESH FRUIT

Wreaths made with natural fruits require heavy wire frames and also heavy wire to pierce the apples, lemons, and limes and attach them to the frames. Natural greens are first wired into the frames to form a background; then the fruit is set in a design against the greens. A coating of shellac helps to brighten and preserve fruits. In most climates, a wreath of fresh fruit will last two weeks outside without the need of replacing any of it.

But inside, decorations require partial replacement daily. It is wise, therefore, to use no wires at all on mantel, buffet, or table decorations using fresh fruits. Anyway, the idea should be to *tempt* the observer, not to restrain him. To protect a tablecloth or waxed woodwork from fruit stains, spread strips of clear plastic under your arrangements.

You can make an attractive table decoration with three ribbons of clear plastic, placed equidistant the short way of the table, over a white or red tablecloth. Then decorate with medallions of fruit, the largest arrangements in the center of each strip. Or, lay a circle of holly with several medallions of fruit, at least four, in the center of the table. On a white cloth, try red cranberries, red apples, interspersed with evergreens; on a red cloth, limes, green pears, and evergreens. You will get a delightful effect, and so easily.

Epergnes and compotes make handsome containers for fruit, especially when grapes are used. Graceful effects can be achieved by placing a short stick through the notched stem of a bunch of grapes to support it inside the container, and allowing most of the bunch to hang down over the side.

Apple Pyramid

The apple pyramids used in Colonial Williamsburg are made with a cone of wood studded with long nails to support the heavy fruits. The top of the cone is sliced off to make a platform for a large piece, often a pineapple. To improvise such a wood frame, use a log 2 inches in diameter, and 11 inches long. It must stand level. Drill holes for butcher's skewers at regular intervals along the sides of the log, staggering each row. The lowest row will hold eight large apples and the longest skewers. The next row will hold seven smaller apples and shorter skewers. The other two rows will each hold seven of the smallest apples, and the shortest skewers.

35

Pierce the stem-ends of the apples, keeping the more interesting blossom end visible. Polished red delicious apples are particularly beautiful. Fill spaces with box-wood clippings and add nuts if you wish (Figs. 10 and 11).

10. How to Make an Apple Pyramid.

11. APPLE PYRAMID. Design by Mrs. James A. Hewitt, Colonial Williamsburg.

TECHNIQUES WITH ARTIFICIAL FRUIT

The best artificial fruits are mostly imported and expensive, but in wreaths they hold their color and, if carefully stored, last over the years. Some intricate work is required in using them, but when small, medium, and large fruits of well-chosen colors are combined in a well-planned design, the wreath becomes a beautiful composition.

37

A good way to start is to organize your material by dividing it into seven parts to fit the sections of the wire wreath frame. If you have only a small amount of fruit, the outer and inner edges of the wreath can be covered with pine cones, or with bearded wheat or barley. If you have enough fruit to make a whole wreath of it, organize it the same way before you start.

Arrange the fruit in uniform groupings and wire it, allowing the proper number of pieces to fill each section of the frame. Attach each wired group to the frame, and cover the wires with Floratape. Interesting rhythms are produced by staggering the position of the bunches on the two center wires of the frame. Centers of interest in each section may be developed by the addition of larger fruits in one or more places *after* all the groups have been wired to the frame. Bows of ribbon may be added at top or bottom. But keep in mind that a wreath is *symmetrical*. If a bow is attached on one side of a wreath, a visually balancing element will be needed against the wall of the mantel, say a grouping of candles on the mantel shelf, or an arrangement of fruit or flowers in colors harmonious with the wreath placed on the side opposite the bow.

DECORATING WITH MACARONI

Macaroni is one of the fascinating foodstuffs now available at supermarkets in a variety of new shapes to tempt the kitchen artist. Wreaths, small trees, candlesticks, mosaics, and figures can be decorated with it. Macaroni shapes are highly textured and wreaths made of them have a baroque style (Fig. 14). It is easy to get carried away with this new material, partiularly if you buy a package of a number of kinds. Practically, of course, you can always use any left over from decorating for a dinner casserole.

Seashells, curls, twists, bow-knots, cornucopias, rings, spirals, squares, and bits for backgrounds are all possibilities. A good selection includes large, medium, and small shapes. The large pieces will dominate your design, the medium size carry it through, and the small pieces fill in and act as background where needed.

Elmer's Glue-All is a fine quick-drying adhesive for small and medium-sized pieces. For large pieces, use rubber cement or Duco cement instead, as the moisture in most glue is apt to crack them. Decorations made with macaroni products may be sprayed all over with gold or copper, or left in the natural state. Brown, green, or

39

12. Frames for Macaroni Decorations. Decorating with macaroni is easily accomplished on cardboard or corrugated boxboard frames. Where joints are necessary, as on a pyramid, use glued brown-paper strips.

turquoise foundations tend to show through the pieces with openings, as the wheels, tubes, and spirals, if left unsprayed.

Corrugated boxboard with paper on both sides of the corrugations makes an excellent foundation for wreaths, trees, and large-sized decorations. Ordinary cardboard may be used for small ornaments.

Wreaths of Macaroni

Wreaths can be made of any size you like. Cut or saw a 2-inch-wide circle of corrugated boxboard. Divide and mark the board into equal sections, and plan the wreath so that each section can contain an equal number of large pieces. The repeat motif is most effective if planned three, four, five, six, or seven times. If you make your design in terms of the largest pieces, the rest will be easy. The design should stand out at first glance. Avoid piling up macaroni pieces without a good strong plan in mind. Think of your wreath as a wood carving, a thing of beauty, with all elements in a definitely repeated design.

To avoid a flat appearance, build up the center of the wreath with cotton batting from a department store. Cut a 1½-inch-wide circle of it to fit the wreath and glue to the cardboard, shaping it into a mound uniformly thick all around the circle.

For a finish, you might spray with gold and cover the raw edges of the boxboard with gold braid. If you prefer a color, wrap a length of red or green velvet rope in and out of the wreath, and fasten the ends at the back. Or hang your wreath against a red, blue, or green wall.

13. MACARONI WREATH. This is made on a 2-inch circle of corrugated boxboard, padded with cotton batting to give depth and
sprayed gold.

TREES OF MACARONI

Pyramid trees made of three triangles—10-inch base, 13-inch height, and cut from corrugated boxboard—are easily constructed. First cut your pattern from a newspaper to be sure of proper size for mantel or table. A modern tree would be made of shorter triangles and supported by a stick of doweling placed in a block of wood. To join the triangles, use brown glued-paper strips. Your construction will prove amazingly strong.

Cover the edges of each triangle first, using the same edging on all three sides. This could be three or four kinds of macaroni in rows. Then for interest, fill in each triangle with a different design so that visitors will examine it more carefully and hence enjoy it to a greater degree (Fig. 14).

MACARONI FOR CANDLESTICKS, ORNAMENTS, PICTURE FRAMES

A candlestick can be made by cutting a base from heavy cardboard, a square or circle as desired. With rubber cement or Duco cement, fasten a $1\frac{1}{4}$-inch section of pasteboard tubing to the center to hold a candle. Then measure off the base into three, four, or five sections and mark the sections. These markings will help you to make

14. MACARONI TREE. This three-dimensional tree, cut from corrugated boxboard and supported by a dowel, has a different design on each side—shells (as here), angels, and stars.

44

your design meaningful. By placing uniform, larger pieces on the markings, you will arrive at a bold design without any trouble. Use small pieces only for fill-in.

Ornaments, such as stars and geometric shapes, may be made simply by cutting the shapes from cardboard and choosing macaroni pieces of appropriate size for each. These ornaments might be too heavy for the Christmas tree but would work out well as wall or window ornaments.

Large decorated frames for Christmas pictures can be made on the boxboard foundation described above, or on old wooden frames. Sprayed gold, such frames would suit many of the old masters' Christmas paintings now available in colored prints at little cost.

Favorite greeting cards may also be framed for gifts. Make a frame of cardboard, cover with small and miniature macaroni, spray gold, then mount the picture with masking tape on the reverse side. Be sure to fasten a hanger on the back to encourage the recipient to hang the gift and so enjoy it to the fullest.

DECORATING WITH POPCORN

The aroma of fresh popcorn is tantalizing! Without placards or ballyhoo, it advertises itself and whets the appetite. A truly American product, you see it wherever there are happy crowds of people—in movie theatres, at the circus, or the ball game.

Popcorn making at home puts everyone into a gay mood. It recalls happy times—winter evenings before log fires, and summers long ago when our parents bought it for us after a big day at an amusement park. It kept us quiet on the hour-long ride home. Popcorn and cracker jack. Cracker jack was the best. First we looked for the three peanuts in every package; then the sugar-coated morsels were crunched one by one, to make them last a long time.

At Christmas, Mother would make huge bowls of popcorn to use in decorating the tree. She used an old-fashioned skillet with a little oil, medium heat, and enough kernels to cover the bottom of the pan. In a matter of minutes, all the kernels would be popped and ready. Then each of us was given a darning needle strung with a yard of heavy white thread. "Two for the tree and one for me" was about the proportion of popcorn required.

Today at Christmastime, home decorators are apt to use an electric popper and instead of decorating with strings of popped kernels, they design stylized wreaths, mobiles, or table-sized trees. Some prefer the golden color of caramel corn to white popcorn. Caramel corn is now sold at supermarkets in family-sized bags.

15. OLD-FASHIONED CHRISTMAS-TREE ORNAMENTS. Tree in the Abbey Aldrich Rockefeller Folk Art Museum in Colonial Williamsburg is decorated in nineteenth-century Pennsylvania Dutch style, with pretzels, cookies, painted eggs, popcorn strings, and gilded nuts. The tip of each twig holds a red-headed pin. Notice the carved wooden animals inside the wrought-iron fence under the tree. Designed by Mrs. Mary C. Black, Director and Curator.

47

Because popcorn decorations may be eaten by family and guests, use the sugar-syrup made for popcorn balls instead of glue. Keep the syrup liquid in the top of a double boiler while you are working with it. A wreath suitable for a table centerpiece may be made in a buttered, circular salad mold with a hole in the center. Simply fill the mold with popped corn, drizzle the syrup over it, and then allow it to set. A white wreath with a large white candle used as a centerpiece on a red tablecloth is very effective. White dishes and white napkins carry out an exciting scheme.

Larger wreaths or other large shapes can be made on foundations of corrugated boxboard. For wreaths, cut a 2-inch-wide circle of board of any diameter. Cover it with popcorn and drizzle it with enough syrup to retain a high rounded shape. These wreaths may be covered on one side only, to hang against a wall, or on both sides to hang in a window.

Ornaments made of popcorn can be made in any shape or size by following this method. Fascinating modern shapes for mobiles or for modern tree decorations are all possible.

Modern Tree with Caramel Corn

In Fig. 16 a modern tree was made with caramel corn. A ½-inch wood dowel, 28 inches long, was mounted on a block of wood. A 3-inch circle of plywood with a ½-inch hole drilled in the center was secured 6 inches above the wood block. Styrofoam could be substituted for this disc of wood. Sixteen holes were drilled in the sides of the disc at equal intervals, the holes large enough for ⅛-inch doweling. The result looks like a wagon wheel. Notch the ends of each stick to hold the threads of popcorn.

String sixteen threads with caramel or white popcorn, and attach to the tree. Drape the corn uniformly all around, and secure the ends of the threads by wrapping around the notches. Glue if necessary. Cap the ends of the sticks with colored Christmas balls. The top of the tree may be decorated with gold braid and a gold paper star.

This tree was a family project. While it was being made, a date was made for New Year's Eve when it would be taken apart and eaten. At that time the dowels were removed for storing, all ready for next year's popcorn tree.

49

16. MODERN POPCORN TREE.

MOSAICS OF RICE

If you enjoy working with mosaics, rice or barley from your kitchen cupboard, a piece of board, some colored ink or dye, and Elmer's Glue-All may be all that you will need to design an interesting wall plaque for Christmas decorating. This kind of wall hanging brings delight to the maker and also to those who appreciate a personal touch in gifts or decorations.

A rice mosaic made on a piece of red cedar siding is shown in Fig. 17. This wood is thin at one side and thick at the other. To a designer, this is a matter of interest. The center of physical balance was found with a caliper (a small tool that looks like an ice tongs) used in making mobiles. A hole was drilled in the wood, and a string attached for hanging. The color of the wood is reddish brown, and the rough side was chosen for its texture.

The silhouette of a Madonna standing before a manger was sketched in simple lines on tracing paper cut to fit the board, then traced onto the board with carbon paper. All these lines were then covered with grains of rice glued onto the board. The face was completely covered with granulated rice to achieve a finer texture

51

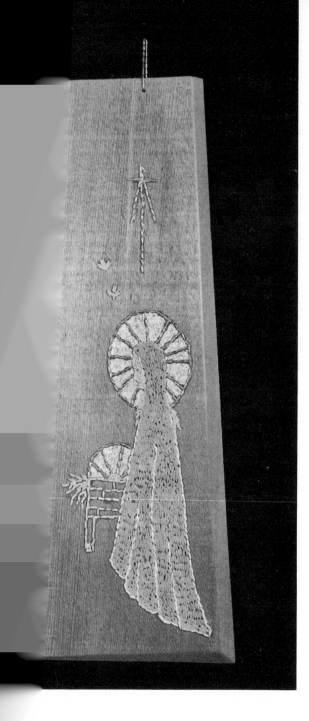

17. RICE MOSAIC ON WOOD. A scrap of red-cedar siding, with edge at right and the base quite thick, makes a background for this rice mosaic, and the roughness of wood adds interest. Off-center hanger is necessary for balance.

and then stained pale pink. The halos and the radiant star were painted gold, the grains of rice standing out in relief.

The lines of the robe were stained with white ink to make them stand out. Then the rest of the robe was filled with grains of rice laid parallel to the outlines, and this area of the robe stained with a mixture of blue and white ink. Care was taken *not* to stain it evenly. With some of the color less intense and the texture of the rice uneven, the robe appears soft and shimmering. The two flying birds were also stained blue. Only the outlines of the crib were stained tan; the natural color of the rest was untouched. The straw and the Madonna's hair were stained yellow.

Workshop Fun With Foodstuffs

1. Cut, bake, and decorate your own Nativity figures and animals from rolled cooky dough. For a stable, hollow out a large loaf of bread, leaving one side open and cut figures of proper size. For a fence, use pretzel sticks.

2. Make a three-shelved table-sized tree with three circles of corrugated boxboard, 9-inch, 12-inch, and 15-inch. Pierce the center of each disc and slide all three onto a dowel, the largest disc at the bottom. Spray all with gold. Cover edges with gold braid or

velvet ribbon. String plain or caramel popcorn and loop the strings in scallops around the edge of each disc. Fill the three shelves with popcorn balls of various sizes.

3. Trim a Christmas tree with cooky figures decorated in color and representing the three kings, the shepherds and sheep, and the Nativity scene. Place the scene near the base of the tree, and arrange the figures in a spiral around it, as if they were coming down a mountain path.

4. Make popcorn balls of various sizes and hang as mobiles. Use sprayed branches for the top of the mobile. Wrap popcorn balls in colored cellophane or Saran Wrap. Or place a looped wire in the center of each ball as you make it.

5. Drape alternate strings of white popcorn and cranberries and hang in the center of a room in the manner of a glass bead chandelier. Use a circle of corrugated boxboard, sprayed white or gold, as a foundation. Or use caramel corn alone to make it entirely gold.

6. Decorate a Christmas tree with popcorn ornaments. Cut thin cardboard stars, circles, and geometric shapes. Cover both sides. Use thick sugar syrup instead of glue.

7. String tubular macaroni of various sizes like beads,

and make into chains, loops, and imaginative shapes. Use thin wire instead of thread for figures or animals, or three-dimensional cubes. Spray or paint the macaroni with tempera paints. Use as ornaments.

8. Pierce a large Styrofoam ball with the handles of eighteen candy lollipops of various colors, or all red. Tie a green or red velvet ribbon around the ball, making a loop at the top and allowing long streamers to hang from the bottom. Add greens and mistletoe if you wish.

9. Make a wreath of large oak leaves wired to a 4-wire-wide frame. Spray white or gold. If white, fill the center of the wreath with various sized popcorn balls covered with Saran Wrap.

10. Make individual popcorn trees for favors for a children's Christmas party. Cover the outside of the cones used for ice cream with sugared popcorn. Decorate with colored cake-trim miniature candies.

11. Decorate a Christmas tree with looped pretzels of various sizes. If you wish, brush with thick sugar syrup and dip into a dish of the candy pellets used for cake decorating. Make chains and garlands of the smallest pretzels by tying them together with thread, or by weaving narrow ribbons through them. Make enough so that every visitor can take home a sample.

55

3

Wood for Christmas Decorations

A lovely aspect of Christmas is the log fire burning bright and casting cheerful highlights on family and friends gathered around it. Descendant of the Yule log, the wood we burn at Christmas is rich in tradition. Long before the birth of Christ, the Persians had a yearly celebration of the Yole Log. They felled a huge tree, cut a cross-section from the trunk and divided this to represent the four seasons. Then each section of the calendar or Yole was burned at the appropriate season with prayers for rain, wealth, strength, health, peace, happiness, good will, and friendship.

Later, when Christians celebrated the birthday of Christ, the ceremony of the Yule Log appeared in many lands, particularly in England and Scotland. In the English celebration, the great hall of the manor, with a

18. HAND-CARVED CRECHE FROM OBERAMMERGAU, GERMANY. This
is 6 inches high with a 4-inch base.

fireplace across one end, was thrown open for the people
all around to join in the festivities. A tall straight tree
was cut down, trimmed, and hidden in the forest, and at
a signal, everyone rushed out in search of the Yule Log.

They dragged it joyously into the hall where it was cut in half—one half for the roaring fire, the other saved to kindle next year's fire.

An aspect of the ceremony was that each person took a sprig of greens, symbolizing the hardship of the past year, rubbed them on the Yule Log and tossed them into the blaze to banish troubles and give protection from the fearful "ghosties and ghaisties." The log was then blessed and wine poured on as it burned. Finally, each took a handful of ashes to protect his home from evil through the coming year. Today, at Colonial Williamsburg, the ceremony of the Yule Log is still carried out in every detail, and in some schools and colleges there is the same celebration just before the students go home —a delightful custom.

IMPORTS OF WOOD

Artistic products of wood are imported in great numbers from West Germany, Sweden, Denmark, Africa, Poland, Japan, Mexico, Italy, and Jordan, the greatest variety coming from Sweden, Denmark, Japan, and West Germany (see Color Plate V). Even so, hand-carved objects of fine craftsmanship are not easy to find, and necessarily much more costly than mass-produced, machine-made articles. But what pleasure there is in the possession

58

19. HAND-CARVED CAMELS. Hand-carved wood camels from Bethlehem are placed in a setting with trimmed, miniature, silver
palm leaves to represent the area where the Christ Child was born.

20. THE CHRISTMAS PUTZ. Nowhere in nineteenth-century America was Christmas gayer than in the Dutch country where the family celebration was paramount and every child played a part. It was a happy mingling of legend and tradition, Christian and pagan. A putz like this with tiny figures of the Holy Family in the Nativity scene is made with a variety of other figures, too, both animal and human, and placed in a village setting near a great Christmas tree. Since 1745, the celebration in and near Bethlehem, Pennsylvania has been famous. Photograph and text from the Abby Aldrich Rockefeller Folk Art Collection at Colonial Williamsburg, Virginia.

21. HAND-CARVED WOODEN BELSNICKEL. This figure represents a step in the evolution of the modern Santa Claus. First came the Christ-Kindel or Christ Child, through Belsnickel (Nicholas in Furs), St. Nicholas, and Kriss Kringle, the English corruption of Christ-Kindel. Belsnickel was a formidable figure in early Pennsylvania, for this helper of the Christ Child appeared a week before Christmas with gifts for good children, but with switches to punish the bad ones. Photograph and text from the Abby Aldrich Rockefeller Folk Art Collection at Colonial Williamsburg, Virginia.

of just a few of them and how much inspiration they offer when we search for a theme for our Christmas decorations.

Suitable materials of wood can also be found in many households—half-bushel baskets, quart or pint berry boxes, toothpicks, popsicle sticks, tongue depressors, swab sticks, doweling of all sizes, thin wood strips or pieces of veneer, and wood beads. There are also lengths of waste wood at the lumber yard. Necessary materials and tools include wire staples, glue, tacks, nails, a pencil sharpener, a hand drill, a small wood plane, and a hammer. For cutting thin wood, tiny-snipping shears or sharp garden shears will do; for thicker sheets of wood, a jig saw or coping saw should be used. And always with a little imagination.

WOOD SHAVINGS FOR DECORATION

One of the age-old delights of children are the curls of wood made by a carpenter as he planes a board. Little girls make wigs of these wooden curls; small boys use them for telescopes. And many a wooden curl has been stored away in a child's treasure chest of "found" objects.

You can, of course, easily make your own wood curls for decorations. Start with a piece of dowel the size of a thick drawing pencil. Put this through a small pencil sharpener. The wood curls will feed out of the side of

22. *Above,* SCENES WITH EUROPEAN WOOD CARVINGS. Deer come from West Germany; foreground figures from Poland.

23. *Below,* FIGURES OF ST. FRANCIS AND MADONNA were hand-crafted in Poland; the whittled wood crosses come from Sweden.

63

the sharpener for a foot or more before breaking off, and such a strip can become a garland for your tree or be used in some other decorative way (Fig. 24).

Yards and yards of ruffled wood garlands can be made

24. How to Make Wood Shavings. A piece of half-inch wood doweling is placed in an electric hand drill with a pencil sharpener at the opposite end of the doweling. Hold the pencil sharpener *very tightly* and start the drill. Ruffled shavings will emerge. A carpenter's plane will produce coiled curls.

25. CANDELABRA, MADONNA AND ANGELS FROM WOOD SHAVINGS.
The curls of wood on this Swedish candelabrum were not separated from the original sticks of wood in the horizontal and
vertical supports. Angels made of wood shavings (from West
Germany) guard a Madonna and Child decorated with wood
shavings made by the author.

65

in a few minutes by placing the pencil sharpener on one end of a dowel and an electric hand drill on the other end. Control the electric drill with one hand while you hold the pencil sharpener *very tight* with the other.

If sticks of wood are used instead of dowels, the ruffle will be scalloped.

Workshop Fun with Wood

1. With pencil-sharpener shavings, create three-dimensional shapes to hang on a modern tree by gluing the shavings to wooden beads—round, oval, square, rectangular. Spray with gold or colored paint, or leave natural.
2. With pencil-sharpener shavings, make tree decorations by gluing shavings to the edge of popsicle sticks or tongue depressors. Trim the sticks with glitter, sequins, gold braid, or painted designs.
3. From a bag of wooden kindergarten beads and some wood doweling to fit the holes of the beads, plan a construction in three dimensions to suggest the structure of a molecule. Paint in appropriate colors. Decorate sparingly with bits of green. Hang as a mobile.
4. Design a hanging Christmas tree in three dimensions as in 3 above.

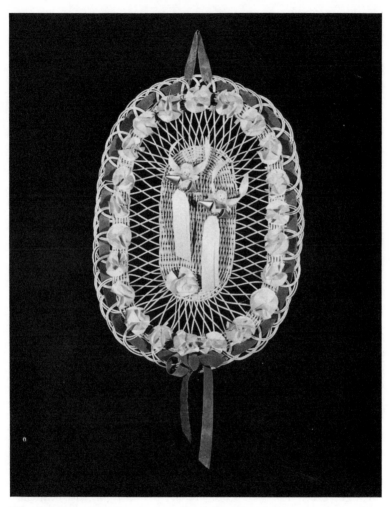

26. ANGELS FROM WOOD SHAVINGS. Angels of thin wood shavings and wood beads are handcrafted in West Germany. Here, they decorate a rattan mat with rosettes of wood shavings made with a pencil sharpener and dowel. Turquoise velvet ribbon trims the edge.

27. A MODERN DOWEL TREE. Two sizes of dowel (½-inch and ⅛-inch) are used for this table-sized tree, 21 inches high. Holes are drilled in spiral formation *through* the upright dowel so that the dowel pieces for the branches can extend all the way through. Here wooden beads finish the ends of the branches. This tree can be painted and trimmed as you wish. In Color Plate XIV glass marbles are used for a brilliant effect. Design by William E. Seibel.

5. Set a 21-inch piece of ½-inch doweling in a 4-inch-square block of wood. Drill horizontal holes to fit ⅛-inch doweling, and design a modern tree for a table. The holes may be drilled in a spiral, if desired. Paint gold or black, or leave natural. Create your own design to fit your need. Decorate with tiny wrapped gifts for guests through the holidays. Reserve plenty for unexpected visitors.

6. Decorate the tree (as in above 4) with small corsages of tiny dried flowers, seed pods, or small nuts.

4

Decorating with Basketry

If in a guessing game you were asked, what household article is used the world over today almost as it was used when civilization began, you might answer a clay bowl or a wooden spoon, but if you guessed a basket, you would be right. There is evidence that the basket even preceded the clay pot, since that started out as a basket. It was discovered that if the basket were lined with clay, it would hold liquid. To heat the liquid, hot coals were dropped in. Or the clay-lined basket was hung or placed over hot coals, and as the basket slowly burned away, the clay was "fired" and made hard. This was one way that the clay pot came into being.

Today, many of us collect baskets, for no matter where we travel, by car or airplane, a basket of fine workmanship is hard to pass up. One collector remarks, "One basket has to be given away every time I bring another one home. I have baskets, baskets, everywhere, but who could discard a good basket!"

THE CRAFT OF BASKETRY

Basket-making is an ancient craft, and few today can equal the artistry of the primitives who practiced the art out of a need for the product. When his mother made a basket of bulrushes for Moses, we can be sure she made it strong and watertight "with slime and pitch" to insure his safety. In Biblical times, baskets were sometimes fashioned of silver and gold and were so valuable that when a gift was received in one, the basket was often returned to the giver.

In the United States, it is the American Indian who is the master artist of basketry. Through the ages Indian maidens have competed to produce the most beautiful baskets, brides being chosen according to their proficiency as basketmakers. Symbols of the sun, moon, stars, animals, birds, plants, lightning, and many meaningful patterns are woven into their baskets. Fine Indian baskets can still be purchased near reservations in Arizona and New Mexico and studied in museums in the West.

BASKETRY AND THE MACHINE

Fine basketry is one craft which so far has defied machine production, for skillful fingers are required to fashion a fine basket. In Mexico and in China, families learn the craft from skilled masters in their groups, and techniques are handed down through the centuries.

In each country, baskets are made by hand from local materials: in the tropics, from bamboo, cane, and palm; in colder climates, from wood—and wood products such as paper—bark, rush, grass, straw, willow, and long pine needles (see Color Plate VII). Nature has always been generous with materials for the basketmaker.

Today most imported baskets come to the United States from Hong Kong, although some fine specimens arrive from countries all over the world. The rattan baskets of every conceivable shape and size that we find in neighborhood stores may also be handmade, but they are usually commercially produced and quite inexpensive.

HOLIDAY BASKETS

As you look at the mats, trays, frames, and shallow and deep baskets in your local markets, many decorative possibilities will occur to you, for baskets are well adapted to informal homes, and especially to family rooms. For

28. BASKETS FROM MANY LANDS. From top, clockwise: Philippine Islands; South Carolina, U.S.A.; Papagos Indians, Arizona, U.S.A.; Mexican Indians, Mexico; Jamaica; India; and center, Korea. Notice the various star patterns and ways of weaving them. All could be used in holiday decorations.

73

gifts, deep baskets may simply be filled with large Christmas balls, shallow baskets with fresh fruits attractively arranged. Mats may be embellished with small decorative objects or with greens and artificial fruits and placed under table arrangements, or they may be hung as plaques on a wall.

To paraphrase a popular commercial, "You can be *sure* if it's basket." A gift in a basket is in some way quite special. If it is a fine, handmade basket, nothing need be added. If it is a commercial product, fill it with something—fruit, nuts, homemade cookies, or perhaps jars of your own jams and jellies. Prized it will be, and long after the good things it carried have been consumed, it will be found somewhere in use.

Workshop Fun With Basketry

1. Make coils of colored tissue paper by twisting strips into uniform ropelike lengths. Glue ends together to increase length of strips. With raffia or yarn, sew or crochet these paper coils into small baskets to hold candies or nuts for a children's party and paint with a mixture of half water and half Elmer's Glue-All, or paint, dip, or spray with laundry starch.
2. Explore the area where you live for grasses or reeds. Working from a library book on basketmak-

ing, create baskets for specific gifts, perhaps to fit boxes, jars, tumblers, or bowls that hold presents of your making.

3. Trim a new market basket with ribbons, sequins, cones, and greens. Fill with inexpensive gifts, large and small, that particularly suit a guest or group that you are entertaining. Gardeners would enjoy garden gloves, garden markers, seed packets, bags of vermiculite, and so on.

4. Tie six quart berry baskets together so as to hang them up in one row, or two rows of three each. Spray with black, colored, or gold paint and fill the crevices between the boxes with cut greens. Let each box contain something different—the children decide what—as tiny creche figures, card cut-outs, little wreaths, popcorn designs, stars, or bells.

5. Make your own Christmas tree with a 6-foot straight branch or a pole drilled with holes to be filled with pieces of doweling. To support the pole, place it in the center of a large tin can that fits inside a basket. For support, fill with stones or gravel. Trim the tree with small baskets and objects made of straw, reed, grasses, or raffia.

5

Holiday Decorating
with Straw

Straw is an ageless material closely associated with
Christmas. It was upon a bed of common straw that the
Christ Child lay, and legend has it that the straw glistened
like tubes of gold. Little wonder then that peasants for
centuries have used this ordinary material each Christmas
to decorate their homes. The shiny tubes of new grain
straw are cleaned and husked, tied into elaborate designs,
and hung from rafters or window frames. Even today
straw is fashioned into stars, animals, and figures representing the nativity. Love and joy go into the craftsmanship, and each member of the family has a part in it. The
father cuts the grain, the children husk and sort it, the
mother makes it into wonderfully imaginative objects.

And Christmas Eve seems mystical when the candles are lit and the shiny straw reflects their shimmering light. Then even the smallest child listens spellbound as the greatest of all stories is retold.

The best sheaf of grain is saved to feed the birds on Christmas Day, and it is the children's happy task to tie the grain to a post outside. This has become a tradition in Scandinavia, and has spread through Lithuania and Finland and to various European countries. In recent years Scandinavia has exported quantities of beautiful straw ornaments to the United States, and displays of straw figures in museums and in gift shops have awakened American craftsmen to the opportunities for unique expression with this age-old material.

Any kind of grain straw may be used for decorative purposes. Wheat, rye, oat, barley, or rice straw differ only in the length of the stems. Large objects require the longest pieces available. In cities, some straw may be purchased from florists, but baled straw is apt to be damaged and to require careful sorting. If you drive into the country, stop at a farmhouse and inquire about hand-cut sheaves of grain straw. Almost any farmer in the United States grows some grain, or can tell you where to get it. Many gardeners prefer to grow their own wheat or rye for craftwork. In most states, rye or wheat is

77

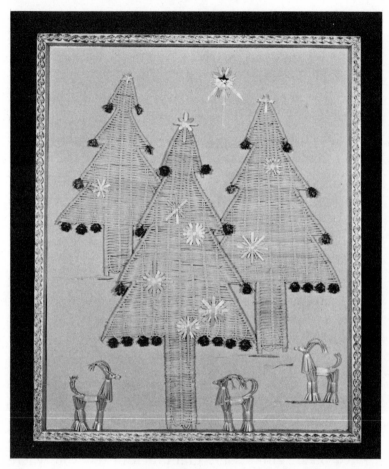

29. A CHRISTMAS PLAQUE. Three rattan trees in different sizes are decorated with pressed straw stars and hemlock cones. Tiny straw reindeer suggest the scale of the scene. The frame is made of ½-inch strips of wood gilded and edged with gold braid. Corrugated boxboard is stapled to the back and covered with blue blotting paper.

I. Above left, CHRISTMAS CARDS. Upper, stencil-knife cut-outs; center, halo effects; lower, magazine-ad cut-outs. II. Above right, WAXED PAPER DECORATION FOR A STORM DOOR. III. Lower left, GIFT NOTE PAPER. IV. Lower right, PAPER-CUP PYRAMID TREE.

v. Left, CHRISTMAS MOBILE of wood shavings and wooden beads from West Germany. The cradle measures 4 inches end-to-end. vi. Right, TREE OF MAGNOLIA LEAVES cemented on a 20-inch cone base of plastic foam and sprayed gold. A tripod of wood doweling adds height.

30. CONE CRECHE FOR THE CHILDREN. A large rattan cone decorated with gold stars and tiny artificial fruits is erected on a
lazy-susan turnabout. A tiny manger holding the Child is fashioned of a matchbox and toothpicks. The handmade wooden
figures of Mary and the guardian angel are from Sweden; the
band of angels from Italy.

79

31. RATTAN TREE WITH OWLS, the author's conception of the first Christmas tree. When Mary and Joseph fled from Bethlehem into Egypt, they rested in a wood where the branches of a tree were shaped to cradle the Christ Child and the ends curled to enclose Him. As He slept, the owls of the forest silently drew near and the stars came out, one by one. And peace prevailed. Here dark blue construction paper is placed behind a tree on a backing of corrugated boxboard covered with light blue paper, and with gold paper stars pasted on. The frame is of simple wood strips, gilded and covered with gold braid. The owls are papier-mâché; the Child is fashioned of wood strips with a wooden bead for the head and decorations of gold braid.

32. Rattan Framed Creche of Palm. Strips of yellow-green palm leaves are stapled together to represent these crèche figures. The wood backing of the rattan frame is covered with blue construction paper. Pressed straw stars embellish the frame.

planted in September and cut the next July. In the Dakotas, Minnesota, and Montana, grains are planted in the spring.

Straw should be hand-cut at the peak of growth. A large hedge shears or scythe is the best tool. Tie the straw in

33. FOR A CHRISTMAS DOOR. A sheaf of wheat decorated with artificial fruits and gray-green velvet ribbon makes a gay holiday door swag.

34. TINY STRAW ANGEL

MATERIALS Wings — 9 fine straws, 3 inches long
Dress — 10 fine straws, 6 inches long
Yellow tatting thread for tying 12-inch gold thread

WINGS
1. Pencil-mark the center of each straw.
2. Push needle through straws at pencil mark (needle holds 9 straws).
3. Wind thread around straws twice, very close to needle.
4. Pull thread very tight; straws will expand into flat, double fan. When thread is tight as possible, tie firm double knot. Snip thread ends at ½ inch. Remove needle.

DRESS
1. Tie 10 straws into a round bundle, 3 inches from ends. Straws will flare out slightly. Bend, straw by straw, from upper section down over the lower straws, turning the bundle as you work, thus covering all the thread. Hold all together. Notice resulting hole.
2. Insert pipe cleaner (with head attached) into the hole in center of dress.
3. Lift one of the straws at the back of the head and place the wings under this straw. Draw the straw back into place and tie the bodice, ½ inch from neck. Tie very tight so that the skirt flares as much as possible.

ARMS Use the lowest straw of the wing for an arm on each side. Bend it forward for an elbow, and tie the wrists together close to the body. Trim ends to form tiny hands clasped in prayer.

TO HANG Tie fine gold thread around angel's neck.

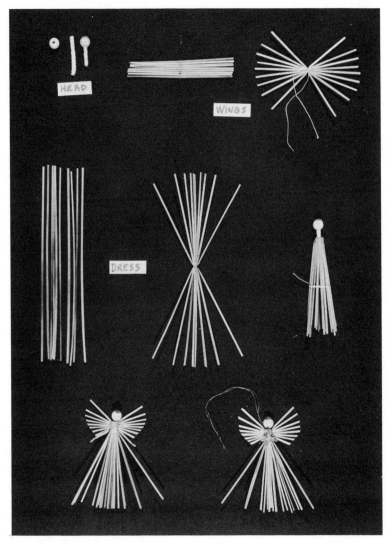

loose bundles and hang to dry in a garage or shed for ten days to two weeks. Then, on some fine summer day, invite a few fellow craftsmen to a husking bee. As you work together, you may be inspired to create stars for your Christmas tree or mobile, or perhaps tiny angels or a bambino with radiance (see Color Plate IX).

START WITH A STAR

Soak straw in warm water for a few hours or overnight before working with it. To prevent it floating, weight it with a heavy plate.

A simple five-pointed star can be made with five pieces of straw of equal length. Tie the ends of two straws tightly together with red or gold thread to make the top point of the star. It is important to tie the thread tight enough to score the straw, as straw shrinks slightly as it dries and loosely-tied threads may slip off.

The two lowest points of the star are similarly made by tying the bottom ends of the first point to two new straws. Allow them to cross each other over the center of the star as you tie the ends. Then lay the fifth straw across the star, and tie to the ends of the crossed straws. To finish the star, tie the five places where the straws cross each other in the center.

The secrets of good workmanship are equal spacing

86

35. HEART MOTIF FOR TREE ORNAMENTS. Straw hearts may be made large or small as needed. Simply match three straws, tie ends, and braid. Tie the ends of the braid together, and crease the center. Turn the crease inward and tie to hold. Designs may be created of two, three, four, five, or more hearts, as pictured.

87

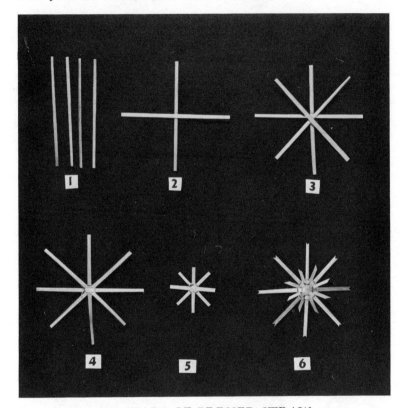

36. STARS OF PRESSED STRAW

1. Cut four matched straws of equal length, and press flat.
2. Place two straws at right angles.
3. Place two additional straws on the diagonals.
4. Bring an end of thread from the back across the face of the topmost straw, under the vertical straw, over the next diagonal, and repeat around. Tie securely.
5. Repeat with four shorter straws.
6. Superimpose small star on large star and weave as before. Tie securely. Trim ends into desired pattern.

88

37. STRAW SUNBURST FOR MANTEL OR MOBILE

Materials   Eighty-eight long straws (18 to 20 inches)

1. Pencil-mark the centers of the straws, and tie with nylon cord as tight as possible.
2. Weave a circle, about 2 inches from the center, with ecru nylon or cotton thread, catching up two straws with each twist of the weaving.
3. Tie four straws into each of twenty-two bunches in the next round, 2 inches from the preceding round.
4. Take two straws from adjoining bunches, cross and tie together 2 inches from last round.
5. Tie alternate bunches together to form the last round, which must be tied very tight to avoid loose construction.

Note: To make a heavier sunburst, simply double all the specified numbers throughout.

38. STRAW TREE ORNAMENTS FROM SWEDEN

1. This radiant cross can be easily made with fourteen straws.
2. Some experience in braiding and padding straw figures is indicated in this charming ornament.
3. The Swedish *julebuck* is encircled in a wired straw frame.
4. This straw star requires forty-four straws and is constructed similarly to the sunburst in Fig. 37.

and tight, neat tying. Cut threads short and trim the ends of the straws. Attach a loop of thread to the top point and hang.

More elaborate stars can be made with more straws and different methods of assembling them. Interesting designs may be composed by laying straws together on a table, then tying the pieces where desired.

BIRDCAGE AND OTHER DESIGNS

Three-dimensional birdcage constructions suitable for tree ornaments can be made by threading fine cord or crochet cotton through three or four identical tubes of straw. Tie the thread to make triangles or squares, several of which can be joined together to make cubes and geometric shapes.

Small angels, birds, chickens, and animals can be made with a few straws tied at important places: head, shoulders, body, and feet. It is a good idea to work from pictures if you are uncertain about proportions.

Fascinating gifts can be made of straw. Jewelry, doll's hats, baskets, toys, wreaths, table-sized trees, and plaques are but a few suggestions. If you like to weave, the skirts of straw peasant dolls may be interwoven with vari-colored yarns or threads into delightful patterns.

Perhaps this Christmas a handful of golden straws will

39. THE SWEDISH JULEBUCK. As one of St. Nicholas' helpers, the straw *julebuck* or goat parallels the reindeer in our tradition. Standing nearly 3 feet high, it is essential to every household in Sweden at Christmas time. It is said that his presence on the hearth magically transforms all children into angels, for if a child is naughty, he will butt them. This figure is constructed of wood and covered with rough straw and decorated with red ribbons.

Courtesy of Zelda Wyatt Schulke.

40. Straw Creche with Palm Background. The animals and the angels are present in this representation of the Nativity. All figures are made of straw, and wheat heads represent the wool on the sheep. A bamboo fence with a stylized placement of trimmed sago palm leaves forms the background. With special permission from *Farm Journal, Inc.*

help you bring into your home some of the love and joy the peasants of old experienced when they celebrated Christmas. Certainly your family and friends will be

93

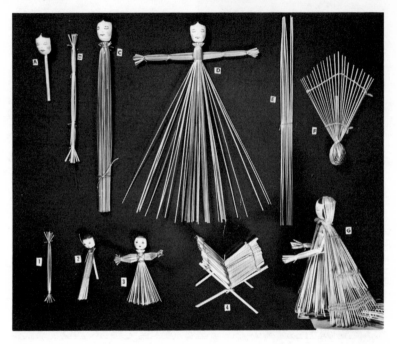

charmed by the beauty you are able to capture with common straw.

Workshops With Straw

Note: Be sure to work with *wet* straw.

1. Make a 10- or 12-inch wreath, 2 inches wide, of corrugated boxboard, and paint it bright red. Cover it with braided straw hearts set side-by-side or in an

41. STRAW CRIB AND CHILD

MATERIALS FOR CHILD:
Ten fine straws, 3 inches long for arms
Twenty-five fine straws, 3 inches long for dress
½-inch wood bead on short stick for neck

ARMS 1. Cut ten fine straws, 3 inches long. A fine wire may be tied into one straw to help bend elbows. Tie wrists ½ inch from each end very tight (1).

DRESS 2. Tie twenty-five finest straws, 3 inches long, to the neck, ½ inch from ends of straw.
3. Place arms under half of the dress straws and back of the dowel, Pull all dress straws together and tie very tight under arms.

CRIB 4. Cut thirty straws, 6 inches long, and sew together on the sewing machine into a flat mat. Make three lines of stitching at 1-inch, 3-inch, and 5-inch markings. Bend into V to form crib. To make a sawbuck frame, tie heavy straws, small doweling, or wood sticks 4½ inches long to make an X brace for both ends. Hold together with 3-inch crossbars. Tie mat to this frame with heavy thread or raffia. Use dried grasses or raffia for the hay in the crib.

42. CHRISTMAS IN THE WOODS. In a framed shadowbox, a Swedish straw squirrel celebrates Christmas in his own way with straw stars, foxtail grass, sea oats, sorghum, wheat, and acorns.

interlocking design. Mount on a wreath of Christmas greens.

2. Make chains of braided straw hearts to hang on a Christmas tree. Fasten the hearts together in side-by-side patterns or in some other way you like.

3. Make tiny straw birdcages (4 inches and without wires), and make chains of these to hang on a Christmas tree.

4. Make straw diamond shapes, and use them as frames for double-faced Christmas card cutouts to hang as ornaments.

5. Braid straws into long pieces and sew together to make baskets to hold popcorn or candy to be hung on a tree or used as favors.

6. Make a chain of tiny straw angels by fastening the hands together. Join in a circle to frame a table centerpiece. Design the centerpiece with a straw Madonna and manger and a shed of wheat heads.

7. Cut angel shapes out of cardboard. Glue small pieces of straw to the cardboard to represent dress, wings, hair, and so on. Cardboard should be completely covered. Faces may be painted or not.

8. Make a long "needle" with a piece of florist's wire, and glue the end of a yard of thread to the end. Allow glue to set, then pass the wire and thread

43. MADONNA TREE. This was inspired by Mexican motifs. The base is cut from heavy wood in an eight-pointed star pattern, repeated in the straw stars. The trunk and branches are made of ½ inch dowel. The straw Madonna and Babe are robed in turquoise felt, repeated in the angel's wings. Stars and birds are tied with turquoise yarn. With special permission from *Farm Journal, Inc.*

44. BAND OF STRAW ANGELS. An organist, trumpeters, harpists, flutists, a drummer, and a pumper make up this heavenly band. Even the pipes of the organ are straw. The organ may be made of corrugated boxboard or wood, painted gold. With special permission from *Farm Journal, Inc.*

45. HOW TO MAKE A STRAW ANGEL
With special permission from *Farm Journal, Inc.*

WINGS

1. Match fifteen straws, 8 inches long. Pencil-mark the centers of the straws, and pass a needle through each straw at this mark. Needle will hold straws until the thread is tied.
2. Wind strong thread twice around straws as close to one side of needle as possible; pull thread gently to make the straws flare out into a double fan. Tie.
3. Remove needle. Trim ends. Weave gold thread on each wing. Do not cut off excess gold thread.

ARMS   4. Use ten straws, 7 inches long. Add a 7-inch wire by inserting into one straw. Tie the wrists $\frac{3}{4}$ inch from each end, tight, so that straws flare out to suggest fingers. Tie each elbow 1 inch from wrist.

HALO   5. Braid three matched straws to make halo. Tie ends to form circle.

HARP   6. Bend one long straw into a triangle, with an overlap of $\frac{1}{2}$ inch. Trim this end to a point, and insert it into opposite end of straw.

BASE   7. Mount an oval wooden bead on a long dowel (7-inch) on a round base to form the necessary standard for the angel. Forty-five 8-inch straws and needed for the dress. Keep these tied into a bundle until the neck ruffle is securely and tightly tied to the dowel. Then cut the first thread.

DRESS   8. Arrange straws evenly around standard. Place arms under half of the straws, through the center of the dress. Place the wings back of the arms, under three straws. Pull all dress straws into original position and tie the bodice very tight, so that skirt flares. Use excess gold thread on wings to make a sash around waist.

ORNAMENT   9. Weave a gold thread around the bottom of dress straws, just above the wooden standard. Tie thread, and secure it with a drop of glue. Trim off bottom of dress at the level of the bottom of the standard.

PLACEMENT   10. Glue finest straws, or thread, or wire, to the triangle (in 6), allow to dry, and tie to the angel's neck and wrists. Bend the arms as illustrated. Attach halo with fine wire twisted around angel's neck.

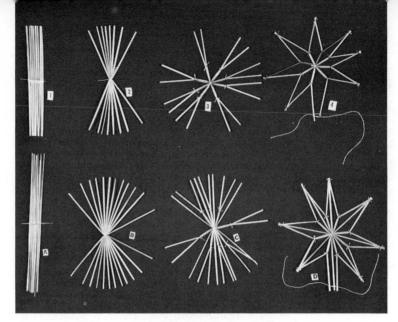

46. EIGHT-POINTED STRAW STAR
With special permission of *Farm Journal, Inc.*

1. Pencil-mark the centers of eight uniform straws, 6 inches long.
2. Wind thread twice around straws as close to one side of the needle as possible, and pull thread gently to make the straws flare out into a double fan. Remove needle.
3. Tie two straws together, 1 inch from center. Repeat around.
4. Using 1 straw from each pair, tie the ends in tight double knots. Trim uniformly.

Variation

A. Pencil-mark the centers of twelve uniform straws, 6 inches long.
B. Proceed as in 2 above.
C. Tie two straws together, 1 inch from center; skip one straw; tie two straws together; repeat around.
D. Let the single straw that was skipped in C become a center spoke for each of the eight points of the star. Tie three straws at the ends, allowing the center spoke to remain straight, as pictured. Trim uniformly.

through various lengths of straw to make triangles, squares, diamonds, and rectangular shapes to hang on a tree. Slip glass Christmas beads or tiny squares of red paper onto thread at the joints.

9. Using the process in 8, make cobweb designs with graduated lengths of straw and small glass beads.

10. Using the process in 8, make icicles of straw with glass beads at each end. Hang on trees or in windows.

6
Sea Shells for Christmas

What is it about sea shells that makes them so fascinating? As children, we were enchanted when a large conch shell was held to our ear and we could listen to the sound of the sea, a mysterious whooooo, a deep true sound that made us shiver. As we grew older, we became interested in the spiral formation of many shells, their delicate colors, and smooth-to-rough textures. A handsome shell is something we all enjoy owning.

An early morning walk on the beach can result in wonderful finds; perhaps right in your path you will come upon a pile of live sea shells left by the tide the night before. You do not know their names nor care, but you recognize nature's pleasant habit of placing a windfall of beauty before you, and you see that it is the live shells that are the loveliest. Although, from the collector's point of view, such a morning's find may be quite ordinary, for decorative purposes a quantity of one kind of shell is far more useful to you than a few rare ones. In decorating, you can do more with a heap of miscellaneous shells if you have enough of one kind to unify your designs.

Live shells must be properly dealt with if their beauty is to be preserved. Probably the easiest method is that of the native shellers who bury their shells under an inch or two of sandy soil and let ants eat the flesh of the crustaceans within. After a few days, depending on the size of the shells, they are dug up and, if the flesh has disappeared, the shells are simply washed with soap and hot water.

Another method is quicker. The shells are boiled in hot soapy water for a few minutes, then drained and the flesh removed with tweezers, or long-nosed pincers for the large shells. A little chlorine in the rinse water helps to whiten shells and also aids in the removal of any odorous fibers.

Finally, clear lacquer may be sprayed on some shells to bring out the delicate colors and to preserve them, but not on all of the soft shells whose beauty is characterized by a white, powdery surface. Lacquering may change their color.

47. CIRCULAR WALL PLAQUE. Cross cuts of the chambered nautilus shell are arranged in a conventional design with sea horses, starfish, and a sea urchin in the center. The circular background is cut from corrugated boxboard, covered with black velvet, and edged with gold roping. A gift idea.

Designs and Backgrounds for Shells

Wreaths, stars of all sizes, trees, bells, and three-dimensional pyramids are but a few shapes that may be decorated with small shells.

Wall plaques, so popular in modern homes and apartments where space is limited, are another possibility. For the holiday season, a plaque may replace a picture and magically brighten the mood of a room. You can make a plaque from a rectangle, circle, or oval of cardboard, thin wood, or corrugated boxboard and frame it or not, as you wish. Frames can easily be made with ½-inch strips of ordinary wood mitered at the corners, and the background stapled or tacked to it. Frame and background may be painted the same color.

The background of a shell picture, or mural, or plaque should be carefully chosen. Color is important to enhance the beauty of shells. Since most shells are predominantly white, black makes a dramatic (and modern) background. Bright orange-red combined with black is also worth considering. Soft greens, blues, and turquoise are good. Avoid tan and gold which do nothing to set off the beauty of shells.

If a painted background is undesirable, try velvet.

107

48. FRAMED CHRISTMAS PLAQUE. A spruce-tree form cut from corrugated boxboard is painted flat black and decorated with small sea shells. Duco cement is used as adhesive. The frame is made of strips of wood with corrugated boxboard stapled to the back, and both are painted bright orange-red. Coquina shells decorate the frame.

This material is especially handsome as background for a wreath of shells (Color Plate X). Cut a circle of corrugated boxboard and completely cover it with velvet. Be sure to cut the cloth large enough to wrap the edges around to the back where they may be glued. Rubber cement is a fine adhesive for this purpose.

For murals or seascapes, colored burlaps (except tan) have proved attractive.

Backgrounds to avoid are natural wood or highly textured materials of any kind since the shells themselves are highly textured.

SCALE AND PROPORTION

Small shells work out to best advantage in the designing of plaques. Large shells are too heavy both visually and in actual weight to look comfortable hanging on a wall. The most effective designs contain several different shapes, sizes, and textures.

When the plaque, wreath, or shape of any kind is painted or covered with cloth, lay out the complete design *before* any gluing is done and while it is easy to alter your design. Critically examine the result, and when you are satisfied, simply lift each shell with a pair of tweezers, add a small amount of Elmer's Glue-All, Duco Cement, or rubber cement, and place it where it belongs in your design—a simple matter.

49. CANDLESTICKS DECORATED WITH SHELLS. Two 6-inch circles of corrugated boxboard are painted black and decorated with shells to adorn antique brass candlesticks for the holidays. Red candles and red velvet bows are appropriate.

VII. Above left, BIRD IN WILLOW CAGE with holly and greens for a
Christmas door. VIII. Above right, KISSING BALL AND SWAGS TIPPED
WITH FLUORESCENT PAINT. The ball is Styrofoam covered with
acorn cups. IX. Lower left, RATTAN TREE WITH STRAW ANGELS
and velvet ribbons for stained glass. X. Lower right, SHELL WREATH
with starfish.

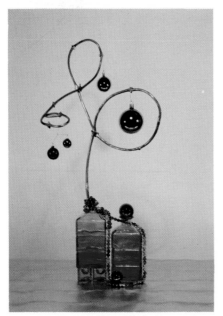

xi. Upper left, LIQUOR BOTTLES WITH GLASS STAIN in an arrangement of twisted grapevine, glass baubles, and glass beads. xii. Upper right, TALL BOTTLES WITH GLASS STAIN for window sills where sunlight filters through. xiii. Lower left, TIN-CAN FLOWERS. xiv. Lower right, JEWEL TREE WITH GLASS MARBLES.

SOURCES OF SHELLS

There is probably no more frustrating moment for a craftsman decorating with shells than a moment when the collection proves inadequate for the project in mind. In this event, don't be dismayed for there are many

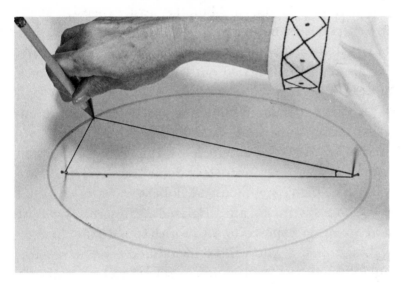

50. HOW TO MAKE AN OVAL. Everyone knows how to make a circle with a pin driven into the center of a board or paper. To make a perfect oval, drive two pins into board, and lay a loose piece of string over the two nails. With a sharpened pencil stretching the string tight, you can trace a perfect oval. The oval is made thicker or thinner by changing the position of the nails. The size is altered by lengthening the string.

111

shops that will ship you almost any kind of shell you desire. Write for dealers' catalogs listing prices (see Sources of Supply at end of book). If you need a particular size or kind of shell, simply trace it on a sheet of paper and mail with your order.

Then of great comfort is this bit of knowledge: it is not necessary to use any but the least expensive shells for effective decorating if attention is given to a variety of shapes, textures and sizes. Most of the designs pictured in this book were carried out with small shells, 1½-inch sizes or less.

In many seaside communities, shell societies are engaged in scientific study, and in the collection and protection of rare types, and many shell museums have been founded for these purposes. Some rare varieties are valued as high as a thousand dollars or more. In shell museums, specimens are displayed against black velvet and are never exposed to sun, which might fade them.

In a museum, you will be introduced to some remarkable names: rice and nutmeg, star, angel wings, cat's paw, cat's eye, turkey foot, cup-and-saucer, sun dial, scallop, button, bleeding tooth, olive, boat, worm, tulip, king's crown, lace murex, peanut shell, fluted clam, and many others. Some hundred thousand varieties have been cataloged. And in a museum, you will see shells in perfect condition, properly cleaned and cared for, and retaining all their delicate colors of blue, pink, and browns.

You may wonder how many names you own.

A family could enjoy a fascinating winter evening around a basketful of shells, each with a pile to identify from a book or catalog. When practically all the shells are named, a plan could be made to mount and frame the shells. Each could be neatly labeled and glued in place and at Christmas, holly, red berries, and sprigs of evergreen tacked to the frame.

GIFT JEWELRY AND SUPPLIES

Specimen miniature shells as well as many common shells make interesting jewelry. This craft is widely practiced as a hobby and as a business in seaside communities. As in other crafts, it is wise to cultivate a sense of design. Jewelry made of seashells can be special or ordinary, depending on design and workmanship. One visit to any hobby shop at the seashore will convince you of this.

Shell, like other jewelry, must be carefully made to stand close inspection. It takes infinite patience, a steady hand, and fine eyesight. Jewelry has to stand a fair amount of handling and therefore must be strongly constructed. Shells are fragile and require either framing or mounting to protect them.

Jewelry supplies can be secured by mail. All necessary

51. HARD-RUBBER CUPS BECOME JEWEL CASES. Available in army-surplus stores, these cups, decorated with tiny shells, make delightful gifts. Lids are recessed enough to hold the shells and they screw tight to keep jewelry safe.

materials, such as sheet gold, silver, chains, rings, clamps, and special jeweler's glue are described in free catalogs. Some shell jewelry is made with sheet plastic, and some with liquid plastic in which shells are imbedded. Techniques are also described in catalogs.

Workshop Gifts With Sea Shells

1. Pick from your collection of miniature shells the most interesting formation you can find. Design a piece of jewelry, perhaps a pendant or a lapel ornament, and carefully plan a way of framing or mounting your specimen so as to dramatize it, keeping in mind that the shell is fragile and the mounting must be strong.

2. At a variety store, examine the displays of wastepaper baskets that might be suitable as foundations for shell designs. Disregard the decorations on them, but select plain shapes. Spray or paint the outside with flat black paint, the inside with a color to blend with a color scheme in bathroom or bedroom. Cut a pattern from plain white paper to fit the outside and lay your shell design on this pattern. When you have worked out an interesting border or central motif, stand back and criticize it; change it often.

115

When you are satisfied with it, glue the shells onto the basket one by one, placing them with tweezers or long-nosed pincers.

3. Buy a hand mirror of Lucite in a variety store. Using miniature pink-and-white shells, decorate the edges of the mirror with an interesting pattern.

4. For a lady's gift, buy a large plastic-covered dish and fill it with cotton powder puffs. Decorate the cover of the dish with a pattern of shells or fish scales dyed pastel colors.

5. For a jewel case, buy a plastic-covered box measuring about 4 inches by 8 inches by 2 inches deep. Cover the top with white velvet, allowing an extra $\frac{1}{8}$ inch at the edges where a finishing braid may be glued to cover ravelings. Lay a few shells in an interesting mural or floral design. When the design pleases you, glue the shells to the velvet.

6. Visit army surplus stores and look for boxes or containers that might be converted into unusual gifts if decorated with shells. Precision-made boxes of plastic and hard-polished black rubber can sometimes be found. Small boxes may be suitable for jewelry, rings, earrings, and so on. Decorate the tops with miniature shells.

7. Glue specimen shells to jewelry clamps and rings and make a charm bracelet for a teenage girl. (Chain bracelets may be purchased by mail.)
8. Make a mobile of specimen shells by gluing them to jewelry clamps and rings. Use a piece of dried seaweed or a sea fan for the main support.

7
Decorating with Cones, Nuts, and Greens

Come fall, we are inclined to hoard as instinctively as the squirrel. As we walk through garden or woodland, almost unconsciously we gather seed pods, acorns, and nuts, despite the overflowing cupboards at home. But it is not simply the need to store that impels us, rather the desire to study close at hand nature's own wondrous designs. Finding a fresh supply, a windfall of newly-created forms glowing with the beautiful color of fruits at their peak, we are tempted to override reason. A child, even a toddler, reacts this way, stooping to pick up a beautiful specimen of nut he discovers in the grass. Finding it on his own, it is precious. It is his. You must find him a box to keep it in. He gives it a name. He comes to know every curve and indentation, the color and feel, the smell, and usually the taste as well.

GUIDES FOR DESIGN

Pine cones and nuts, natural aspects of bounty and generosity, have long been associated with Christmas. Seeing these symbols on our doors, who can doubt there is a hearty welcome within. So most designers think first of these, and in recent years they have added seed pods as well. Inevitably decorations are limited by supplies on hand. However, a short supply may be a boon in working out a good design. Often an over-supply results in the use of too many varieties or too many pieces for one composition.

In making any design, try to keep in mind the two principles of Unity and Dominance. You may achieve both, and at the same time, by selecting the largest elements first and placing them importantly; or by developing the largest area of the design first with just one or two kinds of material. Every dressmaker knows this basic rule for cutting out a dress: "Cut the largest piece of the pattern first." If you will aways work first on the largest piece or area in your design, you will automatically be off to a good start.

In the macaroni wreath in Fig. 13, Unity and Domin-

119

ance were achieved with a predominance of shell-shaped macaroni in several sizes, the largest in the center forming a serpentine path, medium sized pieces around the outer edge, and smaller shapes used as fill-in.

Unity and Dominance can also be achieved in wreaths with backgrounds of fresh pine, holly, or large cones of one kind. Piñon cones used with the solid side to the front, large cigar-shaped spruce cones, and white-pine cones are especially good.

In the making of a wreath, also consider Balance. It is achieved by the sensitive placement of forms and textures. Here again, if the largest pieces are placed first and you have a feeling that there is now visual balance, the smaller pieces will give you no trouble.

Effects with Fresh Greens

Fresh-cut greens work magical effects at Christmas. To many of us they are evidence of everlasting life. Since evergreens are included in the plantings around most northern homes, or are available at open-air markets, there is seldom any difficulty in obtaining a supply for the holidays.

Swags, wreaths, and arrangements are commonly made of fresh greens. But you can anticipate the rush of the season by making your cone and pod wreaths in the fall and adding the fresh background greens just before Christmas.

Long-needled pine and yew hold up far better in wreaths than short-needled hemlock or spruce. Broadleaf evergreens are also good. In frigid areas, florists can supply magnolia, rhododendron, leucothoe, and laurel (see Color Plate VI).

PALM IN THE SOUTH

In southern climates, the palm tree is a favorite for Christmas decorating, and Southerners point out that in Bethlehem where Christ was born the palm was the common tree, not the pine. Sometimes live palm trees are decorated with chains of colored lights or flood-lighted the same way Northerners light their outdoor spruces and pines. Trees are also decorated with natural seed clusters, blossoms, or palm spathes, or with balls, balloons, bells, and stars. To keep from damaging live trees, lights are strung under the midrib of each palm frond, and stars and other ornaments are not attached to new tips or unopened center buds.

FRESH MATERIALS FOR CHRISTMAS CARDS

Many natural products offer readymade shapes for use as Christmas symbols. A small cutting of pine, spruce, hemlock, boxwood, or arborvitae can print a hundred cards. Notice how many of these cuttings look like trees. Tips of ferns are also tree-shaped. Cards may be designed to represent complete trees or swaying branches. If designs are printed on white paper, a snow scene is suggested.

Monoprinting

This method of making prints is popular among artists who want their Christmas messages to be personal, unique. Monoprinting is easy to do and can be carried out in several colors. Simply apply a little paint or ink directly to a leaf. Then press it like a rubber stamp, paint-side-down, onto a sheet of paper. Or glue leaves to a block of wood, inked with a rubber roller (brayer) or painted with a brush, and then press the block onto the paper. Or simply hold the paper over the object and rub with a wax crayon until an impression emerges. The fascination of this kind of printing is that each impression is unique.

All you need for monoprinting your Christmas cards

are a few evergreen cuttings, some tempera water-color paints, a small brush, and white manila paper cut and folded the size you want. Use scraps of paper for trial designs.

THE DESIGNING OF CARDS

If you like to experiment, you will produce a dozen designs in a very short time. Be your own critic. Simply place your cuttings on several folded cards and choose the most attractive layout.

Before printing, remove excess needles or leaves from the cuttings. Reduce each one to a single flat layer. Use a sharp knife to thin down the midrib if necessary. Then lightly brush paint onto the cutting and place it paint-side-down on the paper. Spread a paper towel over the cutting and press or rub lightly to absorb excess paint. Make several experimental designs with two or three colors, or different shades of one color, as three or more greens: olive-green, yellow-green, blue-green.

Artists seldom use paint straight from bottle or tube because the colors are too raw and harsh. To soften the green, try adding a bit of orange, red-orange, yellow, blue, or a drop of white or black. By adding these in different amounts, several greens will emerge that can be beautifully combined on a Christmas card.

Mix your paints in a muffin pan, and mix enough to

print all your cards. When you mix a color that is particularly pleasing, do stop. Then in another cup, starting with the original green, make different additions to get a contrasting green. The third hue may be one of the bright orange-reds to be used in small areas as accent, or it may be a third green, a red-brown, or black.

If you plan to print fifty or a hundred cards, spread the folded sheets across a counter in your kitchen or on card tables. Plan to print one shape and color on all the cards before choosing the next shape and color. If you have settled on a good design before starting, your production line will be a lot of fun.

Skeletonized Leaves for Cards

If you are a nature-scavenger, no doubt you have discovered skeletonized leaves. Among thousands upon thousands of leaves that fall, some undergo changes that cause them to lose their fleshiness and retain only the vein and cell structure. Sometimes insects like the Japanese beetle devour the flesh of leaves, leaving the framework. Such skeletonized leaves must be dried soon after this happens for the fragile lacy shell soon decays. This makes very precious the ones we find on the garden path.

As an artist, you will pause to examine the loveliness of this example of natural lace, finer than any made by man or machine, and more intricate. And wonder of wonders, no two leaves however similar are ever exactly alike.

Many of us have tried to discover nature's way of skeletonizing leaves so that we may utilize this beauty, especially in Christmas cards. One thing was apparent in early experiments. The greener the leaves, the easier it was to remove the flesh. Also, the leaves must have vein substance stronger than that of spinach or chrysanthemum leaves. Tree leaves, shrub, and some house-plant leaves have sufficiently strong vein structures to hold up. The best leaves are ash, beach, and redbud, and leaves of similar substance. Oak and magnolia were most resistant to our methods.

If you get the urge to experiment in midwinter when fresh leaves are unavailable, dig in the compost where leaves were tossed in layers and pressed flat against each other. Many of these will be perfect, astonishingly preserved in spite of being wet for months.

Techniques of Skeletonizing

Take a tip from nature herself for your first experiment. Just soak a variety of leaves in a pan of muddy water in a warm place. Let stand for a week, then examine them. Some will show signs of decay, others may not. If decay has begun, remove a leaf and place it on a plate with a little water in it. Go over the surface with a small paintbrush and the remaining pulp will separate from the cells and veins. Change the water as needed. When you have succeeded in removing most of the pulp, press the leaf in a magazine or telephone book for a day or two until it is dry.

A second method is quicker, but the results are coarser. This method is excellent if leaves are to be used for stencils. The poinsettia leaf from a house plant has proved to be a good subject for this experiment. You will need a hair brush with animal hair, a clothesbrush, or a shoe brush for this work. (Nylon or synthetic brushes are too harsh.) Use a piece of Wilton carpet or a clean burlap bag folded into four layers as a pad. Place the leaf face-down on the pad, and tap the underside gently with the brush. Each tap will pierce the leaf with tiny holes, which gradually break down the flesh and cell structure. Move the brush around so that the breakdown is evenly distributed. After a few minutes of gentle tapping, the desired result will be evident. Press the skeletonized leaf until dry.

A third method requires soap. Dissolve 3 tablespoons of powdered soap or detergent in 1 quart of water in a porcelain pan; simmer the leaves in this solution for

30 minutes or longer. Watch to avoid boiling dry. As in the first experiment, some of the leaves will immediately begin to lose flesh while others will resist. Allow leaves to remain in the solution overnight or longer. Remove one leaf and place it on a plate with a little clear water. Then proceed to brush away the remaining soft pulp. The finest of cell structure will remain. It will be almost colorless. The veins will stand out as a supporting linear structure . . . a fascinating design to study.

The fourth method requires chemicals. Mix 1 table-spoonful of calcium hydroxide, 2 tablespoonfuls of sodium carbonate, with 3 pints of water in a porcelain pan. Simmer at low heat for 30 minutes or more. Then proceed as described above.

CARDS WITH SKELETONIZED LEAVES

Christmas cards with skeletonized leaves delight both sender and recipient for the greeting is unusual. The cards in Fig. 52 were made with skeletonized leaves decorated with bits of colored foil, sequins, and ir-regularly cut tiny pieces of discarded Christmas cards imprinted with designs in red and gold, some embossed, all glued to the underside of each leaf. Then the leaf was glued to the face of a folded white card. The result—a very personal greeting in excellent modern design.

127

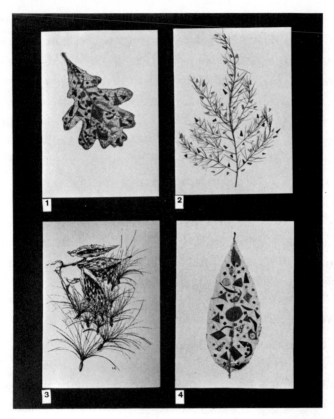

52: NATURAL FORMS FOR CHRISTMAS CARDS. 1. and 4. Skeletonized leaves are decorated with bits of cut foil and cut-up Christmas cards, then glued to cards. The see-through quality is charming. 2. A spray of fine-textured grass is glued to a white card and decorated with bits of colored paper. These three by Mary E. Ferraro. 3. A drawing of milkweed pods and seeds to suggest "Joy" is designed by Dorothy W. Riester. When the envelope is opened, some of the wilkweed down escapes into the room, a pleasant surprise.

Leaves also may be sprayed gold or silver and glued to a rectangle of turquoise or royal-blue paper-back foil to top a folded white card. Experiment with various colored foils for stunning effects.

DESIGNING FROM NATURE

It may be of help to those of you who are unfamiliar with design terminology to have some explanation here of the different kinds of designs that may be used in creating greeting cards. Some of you will prefer one kind, others a completely different manner of expression. The design created for your own cards should be as personal as the notes you inscribe to accompany them.

NATURALISTIC

This is an art term denoting an apparently exact, uncontrived duplication of a natural object, such as a photograph taken with the idea of a "true-to-life" representation rather than an artistic arrangement of it. Photographs made into greeting cards have always been popular where children and animals are included in the picture. Very often large families that live great distances apart find such greeting cards a wonderful pictorial record of the year-by-year changes that take place. Many

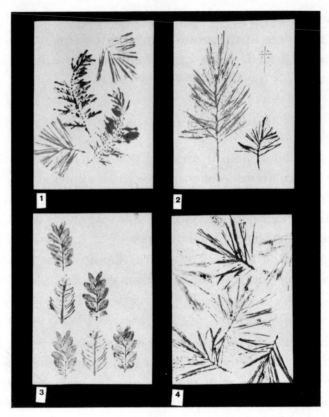

53. MONOPRINTED CHRISTMAS CARDS. 1. Pine and arbovitae cuttings are painted in two shades of green and pressed against a card. 2. Pine cuttings, painted green and pressed against a card, are splattered with bright orange-red paint. 3. Boxwood and spruce cuttings are painted three shades of green and pressed against a card. 4. Pine cuttings in an allover design that goes over the edge are painted two shades of green, with a little orange-red touched at random after the printing is finished.

such illustrated greetings are supplemented by a printed newsletter with pertinent facts of births, marriages, graduations, and other important information. This is certainly a "natural" form of expression.

Botanical drawings found in text books are also good examples of naturalistic representation. Detail is always precise and true.

REALISTIC

This art term implies that some arranging, composing, or designing is involved. On a greeting card, a tree designed realistically would look like a tree, a poinsettia like a true poinsettia, and a Santa like a real Santa, but even more so because some manipulation or exaggeration of lines, shape, or color was purposely "designed" to point up the characteristics of each subject. Colors chosen would be "real" colors, as they appear in nature.

STYLIZED

Stylization is an art term that sidesteps the naturalistic or realistic. If it can be imagined that the tree (or poinsettia, or Santa) were made of a sheet of elastic material and you could stretch it to fit the space of your card, this would be one way of making a stylized design. Hence, the proportions are changed, the outlines are simplified, but the object still retains its basic characteristics. Some forms in nature grow in a somewhat stylized way, as the southern red oak leaf. A northerner seeing this leaf for the first time would think that someone had trimmed away part of the leaf to give it more "style." Stylization may also involve taking liberties, such as the embellishment on the palm tree's trunk in Fig. 54. Imagination is required in this kind of designing. Subdued, rich colors are chosen for stylized designs. Stylizing is not necessarily a contemporary device—many ancient artists practiced it.

CONVENTIONAL

Although the term conventional may imply old-style, mechanical, unimaginative designing, it also denotes repetition, formal balance or symmetry; however, the symmetrical design may also be of an informal nature. Many of us learned symmetrical designing in high school with the aid of a straight-edged mirror held against a line drawing, thus reflecting dozens of symmetrical designs as the mirror was moved. When we found a "design" or pattern that looked interesting, we held the mirror in position until half of the design was traced onto thin paper, which was then folded where the mirror rested, and the matching half was carefully traced. Fig. 55 was made in this way from the top of the palm tree in Fig. 54. The six-pointed snowflake and many star

54. STYLIZED PALM TREE.
Created for a personal
greeting card "from the
Southland," the design is
sketched on tracing paper,
traced with white carbon
paper onto black scratch-
board. (Scratchboard, from
art stores, is a kind of cardboard washed with white
clay.) The artist paints it
with black India ink and
etches with a phonograph
needle to secure white lines.
A similar effect may be obtained with white ink and
a croquill pen on black
paper.

shapes are conventional designs. Color choices for conventional designs need not be bold or dramatic.

GEOMETRIC

This kind of designing may appeal to those who like to work with ruler and compass. A geometric design translates a tree (or a poinsettia, or a Santa) into a composition of squares, circles, ovals, lines, or triangles. Imagination is required to make the design interesting. From a realistic or stylized study of the object, the designer chooses some identifying characteristic. For instance, the radial arrangement of the leaves of the palm tree in Fig. 54 were translated in Fig. 56 into angular fat and thin lines radiating from two small concentric circles. The tree trunk was reduced to horizontal lines within the tapering verticals. Also, the tree trunk in Fig. 52 illustrates geometric patterning. Bold color contrasts may be used effectively in geometric designs.

ABSTRACT

In the geometric style of designing, we approach the kind of thinking necessary in abstract designing. However, the abstract designer is not limited to triangles and circles or geometric shapes. But he does think in terms of simplification of symbols; he looks for the "essence of

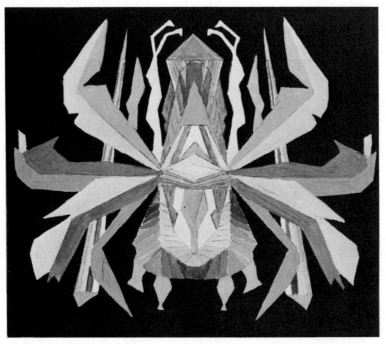

55. Conventional Design of Palm Tree. This design was taken from the palm tree in Fig. 54 by holding a straight-edged mirror in a certain position at the top. A few line-endings are added to finish off the design. Oddly, the result when held in a horizontal position, resembles some insect of the South.

the thing." The designer of Christmas cards is required to think imaginatively, and his own personal feelings become a part of the design. Any symbol of Christmas may be designed abstractly by the free use of shapes, lines, colors, and textures, according to the attitude of the designer. A purposeful misplacement of parts of a tree (or a poinsettia, or a Santa) if well designed could be an effective device. But care should be taken not to lose the symbol in the design. Distortion may also be utilized effectively. In good abstract designing the artist is completely liberated from traditional methods and feels strongly the message he wishes to convey.

NONOBJECTIVE

In this category, no subject matter is evident. The designer simply utilizes color and nameless shapes and lines to create a mood or to express an idea. His work is completely imaginative. Greeting cards designed in this manner might be made with cut or torn pieces of colored tissue papers glued and crushed, folded, or overlapped to present a gay composition. A knowledge of good design is helpful to avoid a belabored or stilted result. To be effective, nonobjective designing must look easy and uncontrived. It can be a way of sending a most delightful personal message.

56. GEOMETRIC DESIGN OF PALM TREE. The radial arrangement of the leaves of the palm tree in Fig. 54 are translated here into angular wide and narrow sections radiating from light and dark concentric circles. The tree trunk is detached and reduced to two tapering verticals with horizontal stripes in various colors.

137

Workshop Fun With Natural Materials

1. Decorate two trees this Christmas. (1) For the family room, with all the old familiar ornaments, toys, popcorn garlands, and so on; (2) For the living room, with all new ornaments made from collected cones, seed pods, and nuts, and in a modern color scheme, using spray paints.

2. Use Glo-Brite daylight fluorescent water colors (Craftint Mfg. Co., Cleveland, Chicago, New York) to set off your collection of pine cones. For beautiful results, have the fun of mixing these colors instead of using them straight from a jar. Paint only the tips of cones, allowing some of the brown to show.

3. From your collection of dried flowers, glue small arrangements onto boxtops for gifts of stationery, handkerchiefs, and perfume.

4. Wrap gift packages in plain-colored paper and decorate with arrangements of pine-cone scales, small seed pods, and nuts tipped with Glo-Brite fluorescent paint (see 2, above).

5. Slice large pine cones into "flowers." Paint tips with gold and fluorescent paint in warm, soft colors obtained by mixing and toning down. Use in dried arrangements by attaching to heavy wire or thin wood doweling painted brown.

6. Cover a Styrofoam ball or cone with acorn cups. Use rubber cement as adhesive. Paint the inside of each cup with Elmer's Glue-All and while wet sprinkle with glitter. Let the outside of the cups stay brown. Color Plate VIII shows a variation.

7. Use leaves shaped like trees for stenciling greeting cards. Choose one large, one medium, and one small leaf for good composition. Fold dark blue, green, or brown construction paper into card size. Place large leaf off-center on card. Dry-brush white tempera paint *outward* over the edge of the whole leaf. Remove leaf. Effect will be a back light or halo. Place smaller leaves in remaining spaces and repeat dry-brushing. If you overlap, do not paint in that spot. For variety, use Glo-Brite fluorescent paint.

8. Lay holly leaves into a design on a card-sized sheet of cardboard. With a soft pencil, trace around the edges of the leaves. Remove the leaves and complete the drawing by filling in wherever desired. Next, take a tube of Duco Cement and cover the lines with cement. Allow to dry. The cement produces a raised pattern to use for printing. Follow instructions for Monoprinting in this chapter.

9. Spray skeletonized leaves with gold paint. Cut foil and sequins into tiny bits and glue to leaves. Cut clear cellophane sheets the size of the small panes

of glass in your door or window. Glue the leaves into an interesting design on one cellophane sheet, cover with a second sheet, then insert into window or door. The see-through quality will be charming.

10. *Gift Idea*: Use a rectangular plastic or wood box the proper size for jewelry. Cover the top with colored foil paper. Edge with narrow gold braid. Spray one or more skeletonized leaves with gold paint, glue in an interesting design on the foil. Turquoise or pink foil paper is especially effective.

8
Clay, Glass, and Plastic Decorations

In our homes each of us is a creative artist, one way or another. We cannot buy everything we need, so we *make* and *compose* many times in the course of a day. The impulse to surprise a child, or a grownup, with something we have concocted—a new dish for dinner, something to wear, or something that exactly fills a special need or that simply *delights* him—that act is the result of a creative impulse. Children especially know this joy and never tire of seeking new ways to use their clay, their weeds and seeds, grasses, or sticks, sometimes working hours on end to produce an object that will please mother or someone else dear to them.

Our need to create is especially keen at Christmas, for during this season each of us tries to reach by greeting card, by telephone call or visit every dear member of the family, every friend, near or far. The more personal our greeting, the warmer our feeling. Indeed, our joy is in direct proportion to the degree of "that something extra" from the heart that we put into the card, the gift, or the party.

POSSIBILITIES WITH CLAY

You could create something from simple clay, intending it only as a temporary decoration for the Christmas season. Yet it may turn out to be so well conceived and so enthusiastically appreciated that it will hold a permanent place in your home—a tribute to your ability to get your "heart" into it!

METHODS OF USING CLAY

When you have obtained a supply of clay from a pottery or art store, it is a simple matter to make figures on a small scale. Guidance can be found in books, at art schools and museums, or from Christmas cards designed by artists. Perhaps the easiest way to start using clay is to roll it out with a rolling pin just as you do pastry. To get uniform thickness of about ¼ inch or less, place two boards of the desired thickness parallel to each other and about 10 inches apart. Then roll out the clay between them.

57. MINIATURE NATIVITY. Unglazed red-clay figures, 3½ inches high or less, were created by Mrs. Elvira Peale of Pittsburgh, Pennsylvania. Notice the incised designs on the king's robes, the feeling expressed by the Madonna, the angel, even the donkey.

With a sharp knife, cut out clay patterns as you would patterns for a dress. Roll some pieces into tubes or cones to make standing figures. Shape heads and arms, and attach these with slip (a mixture of clay and water) to form a bond. Use popsicle sticks to smooth the joined seams, and carve out features with a sharpened stick or toothpick. Robes may be incised with designs to represent embroidery, and the hair marked to give texture.

143

58. FROM MEXICO. Primitive craftsmen of Ajijic, Jalisco, Mexico, designed these organ-cactus forms of Christmas trees in clay, and paint them green with red balls. Handmade cloth figures come from the same area.

Figures made in this way may be fired or not, as you wish. They may be painted or glazed, or left as natural clay. Then, they will look well in compositions with rough-textured wood, burlap, and with greens and other natural material as backgrounds.

WATER PUTTY

Water putty, an easy substitute for clay, is a plastic repair material in powder form obtainable from hardware or lumber dealers. Simply mix the powder with water. It stiffens in about 30 minutes and may then be shaped or molded like putty. A small amount of vinegar retards the hardening. The material is cream color and may be mixed with tempera water colors for variety. When dry, it looks much like clay. A thin mixture may be poured over glass bottles or used to resurface old clay containers. Pickle bottles or liquor bottles have the appearance of clay if covered with this colored water putty.

You can decorate the surface while it is wet with overall designs of seeds, such as watermelon or squash, pressed at regular intervals into the putty and allowed to remain there until the surface is dry. Then if you want the seeds to remain permanently, you can paint the surface of the bottle with Elmer's Glue-All. This gives the appearance of glazed clay. Other textures may be incised into the water putty with combs or sharp instruments.

SALT AND CORNSTARCH CERAMICS

A wonderfully plastic material with which to mold figures can be made from salt and cornstarch. This mixture has been used for generations to mold small objects like beads. It is a clean and soft to work with and as easy as pastry to roll out. It can be tinted with food coloring, dye, or tempera water-color paint.

The proportions are flexible, but these have been found satisfactory: ½ cup cornstarch dissolved in ⅓ cup water in a bowl. In a separate pan, mix 1 cup salt and ⅓ cup water and heat, stirring constantly until brine starts to bubble. Remove from the stove, and stir in the cornstarch solution. Stir hard until mixture is stiff enough to be kneaded. Knead until smooth.

This mixture can be kept for long periods in an airtight plastic bag. It will not sour or deteriorate. When objects made of it are dried out, they will be pure white. If colors are desired, experiment with small portions of the wet mixture by kneading drops of color into each one.

Small objects may be made by molding and shaping the mixture in your hands as you would regular clay. Large objects are better made with rolled-out sheets cut into sections to fit a basic support, as a wood or tin box.

Half-inch tiles may also be cut and used as mosaics. Rectangles and long strips will produce any design desired. Plywood plaques may be decorated with geometric or realistic shapes.

Due to the nature of this material, objects will not withstand weather or washing.

Salt-cornstarch tiles or other objects may be glazed with Elmer's Glue-All, or with three coats of shellac. Either surfacing gives a finish similar to real ceramic tile, and also resistance to moisture.

GLASS AND PLASTICS

There was a time when glass was a precious commodity in the United States. Our first cars had not glass but isinglass curtains that had to be buckled on when rain or storm threatened. Our great grandparents preserved their pickles and other foods in crockery, not glass, and until recently most beverages sold in glass bottles at supermarkets required cash deposits. Glass is still expensive to manufacture.

Now plastics that look much like glass are filling the same requirements and are much less costly to produce. In some cases, plastics prove superior. Although not entirely shatter-proof, articles of plastic are less apt to break

147

59. CLAY AND CLOTH SANTAS. A variety of Santas, large and small, displayed in the Abby Aldrich Rockefeller American Folk Art Museum, Williamsburg, Virginia.

if dropped or jarred by heavy use. Glass requires a high temperature to make it bend or liquefy; plastic, only low heat. When this is understood, both materials may be used more intelligently for many decorations, modern or traditional.

GLASS MARBLES

A common article in a small boy's pocket is a glass marble, and many flower arrangers also use glass marbles in low containers to cover the pinholders. You can convert either of these marbles into glass "jewels" by heating a pan of them in an oven at 500 degrees for 20 minutes. Then plunge the hot marbles into a pan of ice cubes. The result of this drastic action is a crackled, *but not shattered,* marble. A jewel-like sparkle results from the reflections of light on the newly-made prisms within the marbles.

These marbles may be used like jewels on charm bracelets by attaching jewelry clips to them with Epoxy glue (obtainable at hardware or jewelry craft-supply stores). Or they may be hung on a modern table-sized Christmas tree (see Color Plate XIV).

GLASS BOTTLES

Charming and imaginative Christmas figures may be created from glass bottles. Catsup and salad-oil bottles make wonderful angels, each with its own form and personality. Take advantage of any pattern molded into the bottle, and make the most of each stripe, triangle, or curve. Use glass flash bulbs for heads, wired gold braid or copper wire or plastic net for wings, sequins and sparkle for glitter. Each bottle will suggest its own possibilities.

GLASS STAIN

Bottles, glass panels, or other glass objects may be decorated with a clear liquid material called Glass Stain. It is similar to nail polish and obtainable at art-supply stores. It comes in several colors which may be mixed to secure variations. This material dries very hard. It may be washed but not with strong soap or detergent in hot water which may cause it to dissolve.

One of the delightful uses of Glass Stain is for decorating well-shaped liquor bottles (see Color Plates XI and XII) to set on a window sill where sunlight can filter through the colored glass. A fine gift idea (if you can part with them).

60. GLASS BOTTLE ANGEL. A catsup bottle is converted into a dainty angel by adding a flash-bulb head, a dry-cleaning bag ruff around neck and arms, wired gold braid wings, and gold braid and glitter on the dress. (Plastic net bags and plastic ribbons can also be used for wings.)

PLASTIC BAGS

Dry-cleaning polyethylene plastic bags may be used in various ways to create colorful decorations. Try folding and cutting them into 4-inch sections, and combining them with 4-inch strips of colored tissue paper. With the colored tissue in the center, fold the strips together into accordion pleats. Twist a strong thread around the center of the folded papers and pull very tight so that the plastic flares out into a puff. Tie together into two-dimensional triangles, circles, stars, or three-dimensional shapes, spheres, or pyramids. Hang as mobiles or use to decorate mantels.

Workshop Fun With Clay, Glass and Plastics

1. Convert a round, fat liquor bottle into a Santa. Use a round electric-light bulb for his head, red foil for jacket and hat, with crushed household foil for fur. Fill bottle with tiny red cinnamon candies.

2. Convert a glass lamp chimney into a gala table ornament by placing it on top of an up-ended brandy snifter (large size). Fill the brandy snifter with Christmas balls. Put an 18-inch red candle in the lamp chimney and fill the space around it with wrapped hard candies.

3. For a ladies' luncheon party, convert tall-stemmed cordial glasses into angels by cutting wings from thin-sheet plastic and attaching to the glass stems with Scotch tape. Cut out 2 half-moon eyes from blue paper-back foil and paste on the bowl of each glass.

4. Convert two round, fat liquor bottles into Mr. and Mrs. Winterpeople. Fill bottles with red cinnamon candies. Use flashlight bulbs for heads, crushed and draped dry-cleaner bags for clothes for the lady, and household foil for the man.

5. Use a dozen or more clear glass, straight-sided tumblers as holders for 12-inch red candles. Place in groupings of two, three, four, or five on mantel, tables, or wherever a room needs brightening. A quick way to decorate in a large, effective way. Add Christmas balls sparsely here and there.

9
With Foil, Sheet Metal, and Copper Screen

Music and the drama are perhaps the only arts that are said to be "played," but it is the attitude of play that is important in the performance of other arts as well. The artist needs to love what he is doing and find it fun. As children, we found life full of play. Out of the way of grown-ups, we made a game of everything. Life was a big adventure. Walking down a city street, we found treasures in trash. We built houses of tin cans and bottle tops. Each bit of found wire was precious. Our constant thought was, "What can we make with this?"

We did not think of this as education—though education it surely was—we thought of it only as play, and the things we made were as real or as fanciful as we wished. But we did learn the basic properties of our materials, and many a father missed his valued hammer or pliers or chisel while we did so. Furthermore, many a rear was warmed when the tools were found rusty a week later. But how else would a child know that a hammer would rust? And so he also learned how to polish a rusty hammer and to care for tools, and this he did not forget.

At Christmas, perhaps more than at any other time of the year, we are aware of this attitude of play, as we become creative artists in one way or another. Now it is our delight to do something special for our dearest friends and relatives. We want our gifts to be personal, and the gift that means the most is the one made by the giver. This gift communicates warmth of feeling, generosity, thoughtfulness, and love.

METAL FOILS

If the attitude of play is to function in the creation of Christmas gifts and decorations, the artist-craftsman needs materials that are easy to find and easy to handle. He may think that paper is ideal but object to available colors, or he may want a material of greater strength and durability.

Meeting these needs is no problem today, for modern industry has produced paper-backed foils of subtle and

155

unusual colors and textures, beautiful double-faced thin-sheet metals, fine permanent-finish copper screening, and thinner and softer metals than ever before for food packages and cans. All of these products, and others, can be utiized for useful and decorative objects and without the need of soldering iron or welding torch.

Christmas Cards with Metal Foil

Paper-backed foil, or even household aluminum foil, may be used in creating Christmas cards. The paper-backed foil, however, has the advantage of stiffness and color, and the range of color is worth exploring. In Fig. 61, Christmas cards are designed in realistic and abstract styles with foils used in various ways. In the realistic designs, pressed leaves, ferns, flowers, flat seed pods, seeds, and milkweed down are arranged over rectangles of colored foil. These are then covered with smaller rectangles of torn (not cut) facial tissue or thin Japanese-textured tissues. Then the tissues are brushed over with a mixture of Elmer's Glue-All and water (half and half). The glue-impregnated tissues protect the fragile pressed materials and give a slightly opaque surface to the shiny foil. Wrinkles in the tissue add texture and depth to the effect. A light sprinkling of glitter is added to the surface while the glue is wet.

61. CHRISTMAS CARDS WITH METAL FOIL. Colored metal foil is used as background for pressed leaves, ferns, milkweed down, and abstract shapes. A glued surface layer of facial tissue and Japanese tissue papers protect the fragile materials.

157

Abstract effects on some of the cards are achieved by cutting foil into triangles, rectangles, strips, and so on. Some are then covered with torn tissues or with punched-foil ribbon to produce the illusion of depth.

MODERN WINDMILL TREE WITH METAL FOIL

Perhaps no decoration produces more comment than one that moves. Applying the principle of the windmill, you can make a moving tree, as in Fig. 63. This one is constructed of corrugated paper boxboard held together with brown glued-paper strips, some wood doweling, and wooden strips for the base. All paper parts are covered with foil. The tree revolves when the candles are lighted.

Center post: 5/16 inch wood dowel, 24 inches long

1 Wood strip for base: 2 inches x ¾ inch x 18 inches

1 Wood strip for base: 2 inches x ¾ inch x 20 inches

Horizontal support, 11 inches x ½ inch

Pyramid: Corrugated paper boxboard cut into four triangles—

Base 10 inches, sides 20 inches

Bottom of pyramid: 10 x 10 inch square

Brown glued-paper for binding

Eight windmill paddles: Corrugated paper boxboard cut with the corrugations running toward the center post: 10 inches long, 3 inches at center, 5 inches at outer edge

Note: When gluing sides of pyramid together, lay pieces flat on a table, allowing the space of a 3/16 inch dowel between. Drill ¾-inch holes for four candles in the base.

> Center disc at top to hold paddles: 2½-inch diameter x ¾-inch thick, drilled with eight holes for paddle supports
>
> Paddle supports: eight skewers or 3/16-inch doweling, 4½ inches long sharpened at one end in pencil sharpener

Drill a hole about 1 inch deep into the bottom of the center dowel post to receive a nail without a head. The sharp end of the nail should extend from the bottom of the dowel about ½ inch. It should rest on the head of another nail that has an indentation drilled or punched in the head and driven into the exact center of the base. This indentation will allow the tree to revolve easily.

Variation

The three-shelved construction at the left in Fig. 62 is another kind of tree you can make instead of the pyramid. The three shelves may be graduated in size from 10 inches at bottom to 6 inches at top. Shelves may be decorated with small objects or with cookies, candles, and nuts.

62. CONSTRUCTION OF A WINDMILL TREE. Strips of wood at base hold wood-dowel supports for the tree. The point of a nail driven into the center dowel rests on a metal washer, thus allowing the tree to revolve freely. The three-shelved tree at left can be used instead of the pyramid shown. Design by William E. Seibel.

TO DECORATE THE PYRAMID WINDMILL TREE

The corrugated paper pyramid in Fig. 63 is covered with paper-back foil, then decorated with pressed ferns to represent pine trees. These are glued to a white, textured paper (edges are torn, not cut). A layer of extra-thin tissue paper with torn edges is placed over the ferns, giving the illusion of depth and a whitish wintry effect. Torn white facial tissues may also be used for this effect. The tissue is fastened to the whole area by covering with a solution of Elmer's Glue-All and water (half and half). Use a stiff bristle brush for this, tapping the brush vertically against the tissue. Allow to dry.

An abstract decoration for a modern home may be preferred. For this, cut foil or tissue-paper circles, triangles, squares, and rectangles of many sizes. Assemble attractive color combinations in overlapping designs.

THIN-SHEET METAL FOIL

Beautifully finished, two-faced metal foil may now be purchased in small rolls at drug and variety stores. About the thickness of art construction paper, it can substitute for this. Its advantage over paper is its gold-satin gloss on one side and silver-satin on the reverse. Effects can be rich and sophisticated. Like paper, it can be folded and curled in various ways.

HEAVY-FOIL DEER

It is an advantage to plan foil figures in one piece to avoid gluing or wiring. When heavy foil is folded,

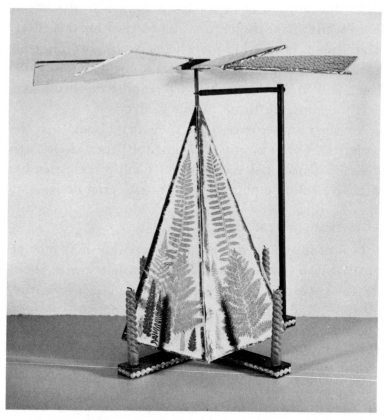

63. DECORATED WINDMILL TREE. A corrugated paper boxboard pyramid is covered with olive-green metal foil and decorated with ferns.

its strength is noticeably increased. Like its paper pattern, a flimsy curling piece of foil will stand on its own if the parts are folded.

The deer in Fig. 64 was cut from one piece, folded at indicated places, then legs and back were also folded to make the figure stand. Feet were made by curling the ends of the legs over a knitting needle. Finished, it stands 9 inches tall, 5 inches at base.

For greater strength, it was attached with wire staples to a rectangle of foil.

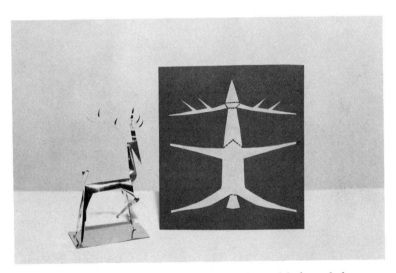

64. DEER MADE OF HEAVY FOIL. This sophisticated deer
is cut from one piece of double-faced heavy-metal foil.

Heavy-Foil Angels

The angel at far right in Fig. 65 was cut from heavy foil. By following the pattern in the center, the angel was cut from two pieces of foil identical to the pattern, and then each piece was scored with identical center lines. Use a dull-pointed wood butcher's skewer for this. One piece is then cut where the dotted lines indicate. The other piece is cut where the straight line is shown.

65. Metal Angels. The angel at left was made in Mexico of welded brass and copper. Its silhouette produced the pattern for the wire-screen and heavy-foil angels at right.

Put the centers of the two cut pieces together and the completed angel will stand.

COPPER-WIRE SCREENING

Copper wire screening is an excellent material for women to work with. If you have made toy animals of cloth, you will understand that woven screening is similar and can be substituted if patterns are simplified. The advantages over cloth are a stiffness that lets figures stand, also the incomparable, glistening texture that suggests the finest of materials for home decoration.

WIRE-SCREEN ANGEL

The wire-screen angel in Fig. 65 is made exactly the same as the heavy-foil angel. Cut two pieces of screen identical to the pattern. Cut one piece down the center where the pattern is marked with a dotted line; cut the piece where the straight line is marked. Put the centers of the two together where cut, and the angel will stand. To keep the screen from raveling, cover edges with Duco cement.

Wire-Screen Deer

The deer in Fig. 66 measures 12 inches long and 18 inches high (including antlers). To be sure of results, first draw a pattern on folded newspaper and cut it out exactly the size you want. Assemble the paper pattern with Scotch tape to test it before cutting the screen. The pattern is made in three pieces. The two sides are identical except for the front leg. The center strip begins at the front thigh and ends below the tail. No strip is needed on the underside of the body.

Use 18-gauge wire to bind the edges of each of the two sides. Place the wire just inside the edges and whip the edges with ravelings from scraps of screen. Plan the lengths of the 18-gauge wire so that the wires begin and end at the hoofs where the overlap of another short piece of 18-gauge wire will give the foot added strength.

The center strip of screen used to join the two sides need not be reinforced with wire, and the edges can be kept from raveling with Duco cement.

When both sides have been reinforced with wire, place the end of the center strip just above the front thigh. Odd pieces of wire may be loosely whipped over the edges to hold the figure together while the edges are whipped with the finer screen ravelings.

66. COPPER-SCREEN DEER.

Make antlers and eyes of 14-gauge copper wire, obtainable at a hardware or electrical store as "insulated household wiring." Strip off the insulation with a heavy knife or shears.

Attach ears and tail with screen ravelings. The tail is simply a fold of screen, and may be attached as shown, or in an upward position.

COPPER-SCREEN KISSING BALL

Three-dimensional shapes may be made of wire screen, as in Fig. 67. Lightweight coat hangers may be shaped into hearts, eight-sided balls, or abstractions for mobiles, and covered with wire screen. These may be used for kissing balls or as attractive baubles to hold candles. Decorate with beads, strips of foil ribbon, or metallic ornaments made from tin cans.

METAL STAMPINGS FROM FURNACE FILTERS

Thin-sheet metal stampings in ordinary furnace filters offer fascinating designs for Christmas decorations. Since the hard work of cutting sheet metal into precise patterns is avoided, you need only cut up the sheet of stampings into small pieces and then go ahead.

Two metal stampings are contained in each furnace filter. These two sheets can be released by removing the

168

67. COPPER-SCREEN KISSING BALL. A heavy wire frame is covered
with fitted pieces of screen and the edges are whipped with wire
raveling. One side is finished only half-way to permit candle
lighting.

heavy wire staples which hold them to the filter. One side is dull gold, the other silver. Either side may be used. Rubbing with a soft cloth will polish the metal. It may be cut into small pieces with tin-snipping shears. As you work, you will be fascinated by the number of design possibilities produced by cutting the metal in different places.

FURNACE-FILTER WREATH

The most obvious pieces to be cut from a furnace-filter stamping are the outline of a circle and two pieces of it which form a Greek cross as in Fig. 6 with the porcelain Madonna.

The Christmas wreath is made on a frame of corrugated paper boxboard, 14 inches outside diameter, $2\frac{1}{4}$ inches wide. This frame is covered with royal-blue metal foil, folded over both edges and glued to the back.

The metal pieces are fastened to the metal foil with Duco cement weighted down while drying. The edges of the wreath are finished with fringed gold braid.

FURNACE-FILTER MEDALLIONS

Six-inch discs of corrugated paper boxboard are covered with royal-blue metal foil folded over the edges, and glued to the back. Large and small sections are assem-

68. PORCELAIN MADONNA IN METALLIC FRAME. Madonna and Child of French porcelain by Liance is framed in a blue-foil wreath against a light blue background. Motifs in the frame are cut from a metal stamping from a furnace filter and used gold-side out. Courtesy of Mrs. Andrew Zverina.

bled to make the designs. Pieces are fastened to the foil with Duco cement, weighted down while drying. Edges are finished with fringed gold braid, and hangers are stapled onto the tops (Fig. 69).

TIN-CAN ARTISTRY

Metal food cans are delightfully easy to work with. Some cans are made of a very thin metal, easily cut with kitchen or garden shears. Frozen fruit juices and some kinds of imported fish come packed in extra-soft, thin metal. One side is gold, the other silver. Unless you want the colored printing to be part of your finished motif, paint over it with gold or silver paint. Spray paint is satisfactory.

When working with any kind of metal can, do wear garden gloves.

The supporting rings at the top and bottom of each can may be used to avoid soldering pieces together, and therefore should not be removed. Punched holes are sometimes an advantage. If a beer can opener is used, the uniform punchings and the metal that is displaced by the punch may both become parts of a design. The metal on the reverse side of the supporting ring may also be part of the design. Each can produces two motifs if it is cut

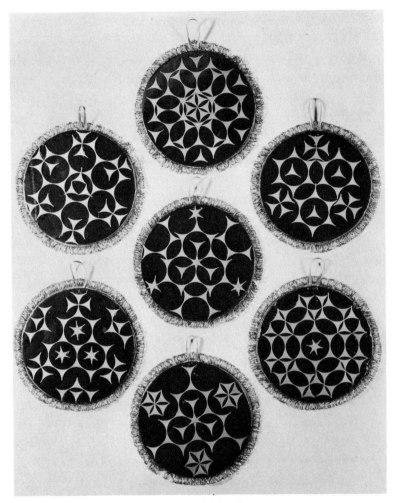

69. FURNACE-FILTER MEDALLIONS. Pieces of metal stamping from a furnace filter produce these kaleidoscopic designs suitable for Christmas or any time of year.

in half. Some large motifs require the entire can with one supporting ring.

Motifs may be built up in layers, making a compound of three or four different kinds of designs cut from the discs of metal that are removed from the ends of cans.

Patterns and textures may also be stamped into the discs cut from the ends. Use a sharp instrument, an ice pick, large nail, chisel, or sharp metal tool that will stand severe treatment. Place a block of wood under the metal to protect the table while you work.

Christmas decorations from tin cans are shown in Color Plate XIII. Glittering metal flowers are made from one side and one end ring of a small frozen-fruit-juice can. Sides are cut into ¼-inch strips which curve as you work. These are wired to gold balls with wire stems. Leaves are cut from heavy double-faced foil.

Workshop Fun With Foils And Metals

1. For an entry hall, make a large copper-screen lantern. Cut six rectangles of copper screen, 3 x 8 inches for a six-sided lantern. Bind the 6-inch sides together with screen ravelings, reinforcing the seams with 14-gauge copper wire. Make base to fit. Place a 3-inch-diameter red candle inside.

2. Make a rectangular lantern to hold two large square

70. Santa Collage with Bells. A Swedish *Jultomten* or Santa printed on linen in red, blue, and gold is the central motif. Church bells, sleigh bells, caroler's bells, and dinner bells are combined to make a jingly wall adornment. The large dinner bells are easily removed for other use during the festivities.

candles. Cut two rectangles of copper screen 4 x 10 inches, and two 8 x 10 inches. Construct as in 1.

3. Make your own large candles for these lanterns by placing a partially burned long candle in the center of a 3-inch diameter tin can, or in a milk carton. Pour liquid paraffin around the old candle until the mold is filled. Paraffin may be colored as it melts by adding wax crayons or oil-base pigments.

4. Decorate lanterns with tin can motifs or stars cut from heavy double-faced foil.

5. Paint twenty-eight or more coke-bottle tops red, green, and gold. Cut a rectangle of wallboard, 10 x 18 inches, cover with foil. Nail painted bottle tops to the board in the shape of a tall triangle to represent a decorated tree.

6. With tin-snipping shears, cut star shapes from several different sizes of the end discs of tin cans. Paint different colors. Place small and large sizes together so that tips alternate. Fasten at center with heavy staples. Use for a mobile, tree or wall decoration.

7. Cut the end disc from a frozen fruit-juice can and also the end ring. Remove side seam with tin snips. Cut ¼-inch strips all around to make a large gold sunburst. Arrange with the stars in 6.

8. Make decorative tiles or plaques by cutting stencil

patterns from heavy double-faced foil with a razor-blade knife (at art stores). Glue cut-outs over red, green, or any contrasting paper-backed foil for delightful effects.

9. Cut a large silhouette of deer, angels, or Santa from newspaper and trace on heavy double-faced foil. Make a plaque of cardboard and cover with colored foil. Glue silhouette to plaque. Use upholstery tacks or small round-headed tacks for eyes or decorations.

10. Cut a pattern for a 12-inch pine tree from newspaper, and then cut a rectangular cardboard plaque to fit it (about 12 x 18 inches). Cover the plaque with red foil. Cut the tree shape from heavy double-faced foil, and cut out stars of various size from the branches of the tree with a razor-blade knife. Glue to red background. Glue extra decorations on tree (sequins, stars, and so on). Cut-out portions will give a third dimension.

Author's Postscript: Merry Christmas to All!

One wintry day when I was a small child, I heard a woman exclaim, "Goodness me, here it is the end of January. First thing you know it will be Christmas again."

And I thought, "Wouldn't it be wonderful if every day were Christmas!"

As I look back on childhood Christmases, I remember most vividly the church service where my father sang bass in the choir, and afterwards going to my grandparents' home and standing around the table to sing the Doxology before the wonderful dinner. Strange, I don't remember toys or gifts, but do recall that everyone, old and young, joined in the after-dinner games—Dominoes, Old Maid, Flinch, Hearts, Five-Hundred, Parchesi, Whist. It was a day of high-pitched fun that we ourselves generated. There was no radio, no television, few gifts to distract us. But what a day to remember!

178

Christmas celebration has changed considerably since then but the quality of it is still the same. Today we admit more commercial intrusion and put more emphasis on gifts and decorations. Christmas is no longer just one day of celebration. Commercially it really begins in January when stores take inventory and offer bargains in greeting cards and seasonal specialties. Many people flock to these sales, anticipating the next Christmas; others make a practice of shopping for gifts wherever they travel through the year. For these forethoughted ones, every day *is* Christmas. They are Christmas-happy all year long. Isn't this a fine thing!

The majority of us do not give serious thought to decorations and gifts until Thanksgiving, when we are reminded that the holiday season is here again. It is then that we are anxious for fresh ideas, and thousands of us go to lectures, demonstrations, and workshops seeking them. In these meetings of garden clubs and women's clubs we feel the tempo of life sharply increasing. At libraries there is a run on books about Christmas traditions and celebrations.

The climax comes on Christmas Eve. Almost everything is ready then. The mantel, doors, and stairway have been lovingly decorated. Only the trimming of the tree awaits the children's lingering departure to bed.

Finally there is midnight service. The church is so beautiful—red poinsettias, pine, and spruce everywhere, pure white altar cloths, a blaze of white candles, carols and Christmas hymns sung with special warmth. It is here in church that we experience the true Christmas. All the rest is just its *effect* on the people of the world. And how wonderful that effect is upon them—not only upon Christians but upon the non-church-goer, the Scrooge, even the non-Christian—as the glad wish comes from many hearts,

Merry, Merry Christmas to you all!

KATHRYN HOLLEY SEIBEL

Sources of Supply

(Write for free catalogs)
Barnhill's Shellcraft Supplies
2310 Fourth Street North, P.O. Box 1300
St. Petersburg 1, Florida

Myrtle's Shell Shop
29 Patio DeLeon, P.O. Box 52
Ft. Myers, Florida

The Shell Factory
Fort Myers, Florida

Southern Shellcraft Supply
P.O. Box 716
Clearwater, Florida

Hollingsworth Sea Shell Industries
Tampa, Florida

Immerman's Jewelry Supplies
1924 Euclid Avenue
Cleveland 15, Ohio

Index

183

Straw Is Specialty of Brecksville Woman

By EUGENIE NORTHCUTT

Meet Kathryn Holley Seibel, Brecksville, widely known as a teacher and lecturer on flower arrangements, decorations and her specialty, straw art.

Her designs in straw have been exhibited at the Cleveland Museum of Art and featured in the Farm Journal magazine. Other magazines to which she has contributed include: Better Homes and Garden, American Home, and Flower Arrangement Calendar.

She has authored two books, one on flower arrangements and the other on Christmas decorations and crafts.

Mrs. Seibel is a nationally accredited flower show judge, vice president of the Cleveland Flower Arrangers

KATHRYN HOLLEY SEIBEL

Club, a member of the Cleveland Museum of Art, Cleveland Garden Center and Garden Writers Association of America.